D1228311

Poems of Doubt and Belief

Poems of Doubt and Belief

An Anthology of Modern Religious Poetry

edited by Tom F. Driver and Robert Pack

The Macmillan Company, New York
Collier-Macmillan Limited, London

The Macmillan Company, New York
Collier-Macmillan Canada Ltd., Toronto, Ontario

Printed in the United States of America

Library of Congress catalog card number: 63-9592

Acknowledgment is gratefully made to the following copyright holders for permission to reprint previously published material:

RANDOM HOUSE, INC. for permission to use the following: "The Shield of Achilles" (*The Shield of Achilles*), W. H. Auden. Copyright 1952 by W. H. Auden. Reprinted from *The Shield of Achilles,* by W. H. Auden. "Prime" (*Nones*), W. H. Auden, Copyright 1951 by W. H. Auden. Reprinted from *The Shield of Achilles,* by W. H. Auden. "Sext" (*The Shield of Achilles*), W. H. Auden. © Copyright 1955 by W. H. Auden. Reprinted from *The Shield of Achilles,* by W. H. Auden. "Petition" (*Poems*), W. H. Auden. Copyright 1934 and renewed 1961 by W. H. Auden, reprinted from *The Collected Poetry of W. H. Auden.* "Summer Storm" and "The Dogwood" (*Promises: Poems 1954-1956*), Robert Penn Warren. © Copyright 1957 by Robert Penn Warren. Reprinted from *Promises: Poems 1954-1956,* by Robert Penn Warren. "The World's Wonders" by Robinson Jeffers. Copyright 1951 by Robinson Jeffers. Reprinted from *Hungerfield and Other Poems,* by Robinson Jeffers. "The Garden" by William Carlos Williams. Copyright 1954 by William Carlos Williams. From *The Desert Music and Other Poems,* by William Carlos Williams. "My House," "Adam on His Way Home" by Robert Pack. From *Guarded by Women,* by Robert Pack. © Copyright 1963 by Robert Pack. All reprinted by permission of Random House, Inc.

GROVE PRESS, INC. for permission to use the following: "The Animals" by Edwin Muir from his *Collected Poems: 1921-1951;* and "The Days," "The Son," "Lost and Found," "The Succession," and "The Incarnate One" by Edwin Muir from *One Foot in Eden.*

CHARLES SCRIBNER'S SONS for permission to use the following: "The Altar," "Calvary" and

«ACKNOWLEDGMENTS»

"Luke Havergal" from *The Children of the Night* by E. A. Robinson (Charles Scribner's Sons, 1897). "Saint Sebastian" by Gene Baro, from *Poets of Today VI, Northwind and Other Poems* by Gene Baro, © Copyright 1959 Gene Baro. "Night Thoughts in Age" by John Hall Wheelock. Copyright 1955 John Hall Wheelock. This poem first appeared in *The New Yorker*. From *Poems Old and New* by John Hall Wheelock. "Wood Thrush" by John Hall Wheelock. Copyright 1952 John Hall Wheelock. From *Poems Old and New* by John Hall Wheelock. "The Cross" by Allen Tate, copyright 1930 *Saturday Review of Literature;* renewal copyright 1958 *Saturday Review*. From *Poems (1960)* by Allen Tate. "Sonnets at Christmas" (II) by Allen Tate, Copyright 1934 *New Republic*. From *Poems (1960)* by Allen Tate. All reprinted by permission of Charles Scribner's Sons.

ALFRED A. KNOPF, INC. for permission to use the following: "The Isaiah of Souillac," "Mariner's Carol," "White Goat, White Ram" by W. S. Merwin from *Green With Beasts* by W. S. Merwin; and "Sunday Morning" and "Esthétique du Mal" by Wallace Stevens from *The Collected Poems of Wallace Stevens*.

NEW DIRECTIONS for permission to use the following poems by Dylan Thomas: "Ceremony After a Fire Raid," "And Death Shall Have No Dominion," "A Refusal to Mourn . . ." from *The Collected Poems of Dylan Thomas,* copyright 1957 by New Directions. Reprinted by permission of New Directions, Publishers.

DOUBLEDAY & COMPANY, INC. for permission to use "In the Naked Bed, in Plato's Cave" by Delmore Schwartz, copyright 1938 by New Directions, from *Summer Knowledge* by Delmore Schwartz. "The Vigil," copyright 1953, "A Walk in Late Summer" copyright © 1957, "First Meditation of an Old Woman," copyright © 1955, "They Sing, They Sing," copyright © 1956 by Theodore Roethke, "The Exulting," copyright © 1956 by The Atlantic Monthly Company, from *Words for the Wind* by Theodore Roethke. Reprinted by permission of Doubleday & Company, Inc.

HARCOURT, BRACE & WORLD, INC. for "Choruses From the Rock IX, X" and "The Hippopotamus" by T. S. Eliot from *Collected Poems of T. S. Eliot,* copyright 1936 by Harcourt, Brace & World, Inc. "when god lets my body be" Copyright, 1923, 1951, by e. e. cummings. Reprinted from *Poems 1923–1954* by e. e. cummings. "i thank you god" copyright, 1950, by e. e. cummings. Reprinted from *Poems 1923–1954* by e. e. cummings. "in time of daffodils" from *95 Poems* © 1958 by e. e. cummings. "from spiralling ecstatically this" © 1956 by e. e. cummings. Reprinted from *95 Poems* by e. e. cummings. "when any mortal (even the most odd)" © 1958 by e. e. cummings. Reprinted from *95 Poems* by e. e. cummings. "Love Calls Us to the Things of This World" and "For the New Railway Station in Rome" from *Things of This World* © 1956 by Richard Wilbur. "Colloquy in Black Rock," "The Holy Innocents," "Christmas Eve Under Hooker's Statue" and "As a Plane Tree by the Water" from *Lord Weary's Castle,* copyright, 1944, 1946, by Robert Lowell. All reprinted by permission of Harcourt, Brace & World, Inc.

CHATTO & WINDUS, LTD. for permission to use the following poems by Jon Silkin: from *The Two Freedoms* "The Two Freedoms," "And I Turned From the Inner Heart" and "Furnished Lives"; from *The Peaceable Kingdom* "Prologue," "To Come Out Singing," "Epilogue," and "First It Was Singing."

RUTGERS UNIVERSITY PRESS for permission to use "Aunt Mary" and "In the Stoneworks" by John Ciardi from John Ciardi, *In the Stoneworks*. Copyright © 1961 by Rutgers, The State University.

«ACKNOWLEDGMENTS»

HARPER & BROTHERS for permission to use "The Martyrdom of Bishop Farrar" and "Complaint" by Ted Hughes from *The Hawk in the Rain* by Ted Hughes. Copyright © 1957 by Ted Hughes.

HOLT, RINEHART AND WINSTON, INC. for permission to use the following: "Answers" from *A Way of Looking* by Elizabeth Jennings. Copyright © 1955 by Elizabeth Jennings. By Robert Frost: "To A Young Wretch," "The Silken Tent," "The Strong Are Saying Nothing," "Design," "Fire and Ice," "Bereft," "Once by the Pacific," "Directive," and "Revelation" from *Complete Poems of Robert Frost.* Copyright 1916, 1921, 1923, 1928, 1930, 1934, 1939, 1947 by Holt, Rinehart and Winston, Inc. Copyright 1936, 1942 by Robert Frost. Copyright renewed 1944, 1951, © 1956, 1962 by Robert Frost. All reprinted by permission of Holt, Rinehart and Winston, Inc.

THE MARVELL PRESS for permission to use "Church Going" by Philip Larkin from *The Less Deceived* by permission of The Marvell Press, Hessle, Yorkshire, England.

HOUGHTON MIFFLIN COMPANY for permission to use the following: "For God While Sleeping" from Anne Sexton's *All My Pretty Ones;* "The Avenue Bearing the Initial of Christ into the New World" by Galway Kinnell; and "A Cold Spring" and "2000 Illustrations and a Complete Concordance" by Elizabeth Bishop from *Poems: North and South.*

FARRAR, STRAUS & CUDAHY, INC. for permission to use "If He Were Anywhere," "My Absent God," and "Witnesses" by Cecil Hemley from *In the Midnight Wood* by Cecil Hemley. Copyright © 1951, 1956, 1958 by Cecil Hemley.

FUNK & WAGNALLS COMPANY for permission to use "Those Not Elect" by Leonie Adams. Reprinted from *Poems: A Selection by Leonie Adams,* permission of the publisher, Funk & Wagnalls, New York.

WILLIAM HEINEMANN, LTD. for permission to use "Black Rook in Rainy Weather" from *The Colossus and Other Poems* by Sylvia Plath.

WESLEYAN UNIVERSITY PRESS for permission to use "The Tree of Silence" and "Fantasy on the Resurrection" by Vassar Miller, copyright © 1960 by Vassar Miller. Reprinted from *Wage War on Silence* by Vassar Miller, by permission of Wesleyan University Press.

YALE UNIVERSITY PRESS for permission to use George Starbuck's "Poems from a First Year in Boston, Section IV: Autumn: Progress Report" from his book, *Bone Thoughts.*

LIVERIGHT PUBLISHING CORPORATION for permission to use "Ave Maria," "Voyages II," and "To Brooklyn Bridge" from *The Collected Poems of Hart Crane.*

THE MACMILLAN COMPANY for permission to use the following: "Two Songs of a Fool" Part I, by W. B. Yeats from *Collected Poems,* Copyright 1919 by The Macmillan Company, renewed 1946 by Bertha Georgie Yeats. "The Rose of Peace" and "To Some I Have Talked With By the Fire" from *Collected Poems* by W. B. Yeats, copyright 1906 by The Macmillan Company, renewed 1934 by William Butler Yeats. "The Three Hermits" and "The Magi," from *Collected Poems* by W. B. Yeats, copyright 1916 The Macmillan Company, renewed 1944 by William Butler Yeats. "Sailing to Byzantium" and "Two Songs from a Play" by W. B. Yeats, copyright 1928 by The Macmillan Company, renewed 1956 by Bertha Georgie

Yeats. "Crazy Jane on God," "Vacillation," and "Dialogue on Self and Soul" from *Collected Poems* by W. B. Yeats, copyright 1933 by The Macmillan Company, renewed 1961 by Bertha Georgie Yeats. "The Second Coming" from *Collected Poems* by W. B. Yeats, copyright 1924 by The Macmillan Company, renewed 1952 by Bertha Georgie Yeats. "What Are Years" from *Collected Poems* by Marianne Moore, copyright 1941 by Marianne Moore. "Goat Paths" from *Collected Poems* by James Stephens, copyright 1915 The Macmillan Company, renewed 1943 by James Stephens. "A Christmas Sonnet" from *Collected Poems* by E. A. Robinson, copyright 1935, 1937 by The Macmillan Company. "The Wandering Jew" from *Collected Poems* by E. A. Robinson, copyright 1920 by Edwin Arlington Robinson, renewed 1948 by Ruth Nivison.

MARGOT JOHNSON AGENCY for permission to use Howard Nemerov's "Moment" and "Boom" from *New and Selected Poems,* copyright © 1960 by The University of Chicago.

HAROLD MATSON COMPANY, INC. for permission to use C. Day Lewis's "Tempt Me No More."

OXFORD UNIVERSITY PRESS, INC. for permission to use the following: Richard Eberhart's "The Book of Nature," "Order and Disorder," "The Horse Chestnut Tree," and "Sea Scape With Parable" from *Collected Poems 1930–1960* by Richard Eberhart. © Richard Eberhart 1960. Conrad Aiken's "Memnon III," "Memnon V." "Tetélestai," "The Room," and "The Sound of Breaking" from *Collected Poems* by Conrad Aiken. Copyright 1953 by Conrad Aiken. Gerard Manley Hopkins's "God's Grandeur," "Spring," "The Windhover," "Pied Beauty," "Thou Art Indeed Just, Lord," "My Own Heart Let Me Have More Pity On," "I Wake and Feel the Fell of Dark," "Spelt From Sibyl's Leaves," "Carrion Comfort," and "The Leaden Echo and the Golden Echo" from *Poems of Gerard Manley Hopkins,* Third Edition, edited by W. H. Gardner. Copyright 1948 by Oxford University Press, Inc. Louis MacNeice's "Hands and Eyes" from *Eighty-Five Poems* of Louis MacNeice. © 1959 by Louis MacNeice. All by permission of Oxford University Press, Inc.

Ted Hughes for permission to use his poem, "Pibroch."

To our wives we owe much thanks—to Patricia Pack for hours of typing and proofreading, and to Anne Driver for preparation of the index.

T. F. D.
R. P.

This book is dedicated
to the poets whose work it contains

Table of Contents

PART THREE — Meditation and Spiritual Journey

PART FOUR God's Death

Preface

Our purpose in assembling this anthology is to demonstrate what may be a surprise to many—that the mode and vocabulary of religious inquiry and expression have remained, even through our "scientific century," a major concern among poets. This is not an anthology of religious poets, however, but rather of religious poems; many of the poems included here were written by poets whose greater body of work is concerned with subjects other than man's relationship to God, man's search for God, or man's sense of loss and chaos in a world without God.

The criterion we began with demanded that the poem, to qualify for the anthology, must at least imply the presence of a God in whose image man was created and to whom man was a concern. This presence, we felt, might be experienced in a number of ways: (1) The poem itself might be an act of praise, a prayer, or an imploration, as if it were a wish to seek out and embody the will of God. (2) The poem might express an estrangement from God, in which the poetic speaker puzzles about the inscrutability of God's purposes or actions, or in which he doubts the existence of God. This question for him, however, must remain painfully open, and it is his emotion of doubt, and the inescapability of the object of this doubt, that moves at the heart of the poem. (3) The poem might also be written in a voice, not of involvement as in the first two categories, but in a narrator's voice which describes some imagined character's struggle or meditation in respect to God. If the author is speaking in his own meditative voice, his address, in this category, would not be outward to God but inward to himself.

In each of these categories the presence of God is felt through his creation, his benevolence or his wrath; or it is felt as a questioned absence, with conviction always in the balance, threatening the believer-doubter with ultimate emptiness. No poem here turns away from the question of God's will or God's existence as irrelevant: The agnostic poet, worried about his agnosticism—unlike the atheist for whom the question is closed—still writes religious poems. But there is one kind of atheistic poem that we feel belongs in an anthology of modern religious verse—it is written by the atheist who, rather than turning completely from the contemplation of God, writes about *not believing* in God, or who writes specifically about a man or a civilization that has rejected the belief in God, that finds such belief no longer possible.

Poetry is not philosophy or theology; it is not doctrine of any kind. Good poems have been made with trivial ideas, and there is a plethora of wisdom-filled bad poems. But one must understand the ideas of a poem in order to understand the poem itself. Although one can never completely suspend personal beliefs in reading a poem about God (this subjectivity necessarily colors every reader's response), nevertheless what one ultimately demands of the poem is that it allows one to believe in the poet believing in God. It is the spectacle of human life that attracts our fascination and our concern.

The poet bears witness to the life outside him and the life within him, and he is objective only to the extent that he is comprehensive—that is, to the extent he can describe what he feels in seeing what he sees. Perhaps it is better to say that he bears interpretive witness, and that this interpretation is necessary, for he is always part of the scene which he observes.

There are those who read the Bible as poetry or as history. This does not mean that they do not believe in God or do not think of the Bible as expressing religious truth. Both poetry and history may point to the same God, and specific revelation for them is possible without literal inspiration. Thus they continue to see poetry as revelation, the Bible being the first poem, the poem of poems, and thus, justifiably, the inspiration of the great body of Western writing which has not merely reused but rather re-experienced its myths and parables which continue to bear witness to the spiritual presence of God. The poem as a social or ritualistic act binds together the religious community, and the poet, in return, is nourished by the continuity, and thus the inheritance, that the community offers.

And for those who, perhaps like myself, have come to hold an atheistic position, who cannot reconcile the idea of God with his own experience and his own reading of history, who, for example, read the story of the fall from the Garden of Eden as a parable of man's infancy and the infancy of a civilization, still, a religious poem, seriously and perplexedly felt, remains a pertinent and moving description of mankind seeking its origin and destiny.

R. P.

Poems of Doubt and Belief

Introduction

THE RELIGIOUS CONSCIOUSNESS AND THE POETIC CONSCIOUSNESS ARE ONE in essence. In existence they diverge. All discussions about the unity of religion and poetry and about the conflicts between them are therefore discussions of the Fall, and this is acknowledged implicitly by the poet as well as explicitly by the theologian.

Northrop Frye is right to say that between religion and poetry "there must always be some kind of tension, until the possible and the actual meet at infinity."[1] This tension is the product of conflicting views of salvation, which we understand here in its root sense as the restoration of that which is diseased or broken to a state of health or wholeness.

For religion, especially Christianity and historic Judaism, salvation depends upon revelation. Something must be given from outside the field of estrangement. It must be given and it must be received. The religious institution with its doctrine, its preaching, and its communal liturgy, is the locus of the giving and the receiving. The religious believer may then try to unite poetry and faith by making poetry the instrument of religious expression. He finds himself happiest with orthodox poetry, which gives lyric voice to the content of revelation or which dramatizes various moments in the life of faith.

For poetry, as such, salvation depends upon imagination. Something must be perceived *within* the field of estrangement. The poet's task is to overcome estrangement by reconciling "discordant qualities." The modest poet, he who is least given to Romantic ambitions, will settle for the moments of reconciliation that come in individual poems.

[1] *Anatomy of Criticism*. Princeton: Princeton University Press, 1957, p. 128.

The more Romantic poet will elevate poetry into *the* way of reconciling the discordances of experience and will thereby make poetry a substitute for religious salvation.

In the present collection, contrasting attitudes toward salvation are represented by W. H. Auden and Wallace Stevens. Auden is not only a poet but also a religious believer. Therefore he knows that poetry, even his own, can threaten religious confession. Auden's great meditative work on imagination, *The Sea and the Mirror,*—too long for inclusion here—is in sum a prayer that imagination be at last transcended by revelation, that "all our meanings" be "reversed" in the mirror that God holds up to the mirror of art. Yet even by this stratagem Auden the believer cannot get away from Auden the poet. The more poetry attempts to point beyond itself, the more it dazzles us with its poetic ingenuity. How can imagination resign itself except to a higher form of imagination? Auden resolves the question through a Kierkegaardian appeal to the Absurd, a word he uses elsewhere as a name for God. The poet asks for an "accident," in the typesetter's room if nowhere else, that will happily upset the poet's design and cause the finished work to herald a meaning beyond itself. By some such means, the Ultimately Real will speak, answering the existential question of the poet:

> how
> Shall we satisfy when we meet,
> Between Shall-I and I-Will,
> The lion's mouth whose hunger
> No metaphors can fill?

In Wallace Stevens we find a more Romantic view of the poet's enterprise. All transcendent sources of grace are denied, while the search for an equivalent of grace in the "unsponsored" world is eagerly taken up. Stevens maintains that he is not in pursuit of salvation, for to him the salvation of which religion speaks is not only illusory but also unnecessary. To live is itself good, and those in heaven, if such there be, can experience only "the minor of what we feel."

Nevertheless, it is clear, on the testimony of Stevens' essays as well as his major poems, that he believes the poetic imagination can and should assume the now-discredited functions of religious revelation and salvation. Reality itself contains no salvation, but the imagination, "pressing back against the pressure of reality," moves toward the "supreme fiction" and so enables man to achieve such wholeness as he needs. Wallace Stevens' "noble rider" is the poet, who through his "sound of words" becomes a high priest of the "necessary angel," imagination. Hence the poet-priest says of the woman whose meditations are overheard in *Sunday Morning:*

> Divinity must live within herself:
> Passions of rain, or moods in falling snow;
> . . .
> All pleasures and all pains, remembering
> The bough of summer and the winter branch.
> These are the measures destined for her soul.

For Wallace Stevens the world is an "island solitude, unsponsored, free," and the ministries it needs are to be found in imagination itself.

We have then the poet who believes in a salvation transcending poetry and the poet for whom contentment replaces salvation within the imaginative act. This anthology includes them both, for the assertion of the one is empty without the reply of the other. The religious life exists in dialogue or it does not exist at all. The religious faith of an Auden is faith precisely because it is aware of its purely poetic alternative, and the secularism of Stevens is secular precisely because it springs from a negation of faith. A meaningful anthology of religious poetry must incorporate both parts of the dialectic.

In spite of religion's avowal that metaphor is insufficient for salvation, it is yet true that wherever we find the urgency of faith we also find poetic expression. The argument is not circular: we do not conclude tautologically that urgency of faith produces poetry because in some poetry we find urgency of faith. Rather, the argument is based upon our experience of how we react when faith possesses us. We are at those times driven to respond to that which has seized us, and our response has the character of wanting to do or to make something that is appropriate to the nature of the object of our faith. The response may be to perform the ethical act. It may be to purify the heart. It may be to form a community or to join one. It may be to build a building, to paint a picture, or to find words appropriate to the reality that has been encountered. In any event, where faith becomes immediate the old things will no longer entirely do. In theology we say that the Spirit moves where it will, and that the received doctrine and tradition are put under judgment. The result is a new form of expression, threatening in one degree or another the religious establishment. When the expression is verbal, it has the quality of poetic creation.

For this reason, most of the prophets were poets. In them faith was so immediate that the rehearsed responses of the community would no longer suffice. Hence the prophetic attacks upon the morality and priesthood of Israel. The recurrent antagonisms between Prophet and Priest may be understood as conflict between two kinds of poetry: that of the priests, which is poetry ossified by time, and that of the prophets, which is poetry fresh from the womb of immediacy. The terrible irony of Ezekiel is that he is a child of the Spirit walking through the valley of dry bones.

What we say of the prophet we may also say of the mystic, whose attempt to communicate the incommunicable leads him directly to the symbolic and paradoxical language of poetry.

It happens that at the present time theology is wrestling with the intellectual problems that arise when one acknowledges the omnipresence of metaphor (and myth) in the utterances of those whose faith strives to transcend metaphor.

In ages when thought was less self-conscious than in ours, the embarrassment of faith did not attach itself to modes of speech. It is when the myths are "broken," to use Paul Tillich's expression, that the problem of language is acute. Some observers will see in this fact only the inevitable tendency of religion to become myth, and of myth to become the material of art. Others will see instead a growth in the religious consciousness, whereby man's conception of God is modified so as to preserve His transcendence in relation to new forms of thought.

Religion is necessarily poetic, and the validity of theology as an enterprise depends upon the viability of its understanding of poetry.

It is no accident that both poetry and religion today must defend themselves by similar strategies against the threatening dominance of scientism. There is no more enlightening pilgrimage in our time than that which has led Mr. I. A. Richards from his early attempts to justify the function of poetry on scientific grounds to his later recognition that science itself is like poetry:

> For while any part of the world-picture is regarded
> as not of mythopoeic origin, poetry . . . could not but be
> be given a second place. . . . If we grant that all is
> myth, poetry, as the myth-making which most brings
> "the whole soul of man into activity" . . . becomes the
> channel for the reconstitution of order.[2]

The unity of poetry and religion may be observed in another regard, one more directly evident in most of the poems in this anthology. The life of poetry, quite apart from faith or doctrine, is dependent upon the poet's astonishment when he looks at the actual world. This is especially true of lyric poetry. Where the poet's fascination and surprise help to shape his poem, something akin to a religious attitude arises.

The dearest quality of poetry is that it catches us unawares and fills us with wonder. Perhaps we are made to wonder that things are, that existence *is*. Perhaps we are taught suddenly that old things gain new life from new arrangement. In any case, we hold fast to the poet because, as creator, he throws away nothing and yet makes all things new. Able to do this, the poet is often tempted to read the creativity ascribed to God as a metaphor for his own faculties, whereas religious faith would have it the other way around. Nevertheless, the poet is indispensable. Where the imaginative power of finding the new in the old is lost, the human spirit dies and with it all possibility of man's being addressed by the divine Spirit.

Some readers, for whom all things are seen through the spectacles of their orthodoxy, will find the life in many of the poems of this anthology demonic. Nevertheless, it is sufficient if they find here any life at all. Our test put to the poems we would include has not been orthodoxy of any kind. It has merely been to find genuine poetry that

[2] *Coleridge on Imagination*. New York: W. W. Norton & Co., 1950, p. 228.

points, by positive or negative declarations, to the question of a reality transcending man and nature.

On the one side of metaphor lies science. On the other side lies a mystery that we sense to be unfathomable. Here are poems that move toward the boundaries of metaphor on the side of unfathomable mystery. So far the human spirit goes. Beyond, there is only the invocation and the unpredictable breath of the Spirit.

TOM F. DRIVER

Part One

PRAYER AND PRAISE

Gerard Manley Hopkins

« 1844 - 1889 »

GOD'S GRANDEUR

The world is charged with the grandeur of God.
It will flame out, like shining from shook foil;
It gathers to a greatness, like the ooze of oil
Crushed. Why do men then now not reck his rod?
Generations have trod, have trod, have trod;
And all is seared with trade; bleared, smeared with toil;
And wears man's smudge and shares man's smell: the soil
Is bare now, nor can foot feel, being shod.
And for all this, nature is never spent;
There lives the dearest freshness deep down things;
And though the last lights off the black West went
Oh, morning, at the brown brink eastward, springs—
Because the Holy Ghost over the bent
World broods with warm breast and with ah! bright wings.

SPRING

Nothing is so beautiful as spring—
  When weeds, in wheels, shoot long and lovely and lush;
  Thrush's eggs look little low heavens, and thrush
Through the echoing timber does so rinse and wring
The ear, it strikes like lightnings to hear him sing;
  The glassy peartree leaves and blooms, they brush
  The descending blue; that blue is all in a rush
With richness; the racing lambs too have fair their fling.

What is all this juice and all this joy?
  A strain of the earth's sweet being in the beginning
In Eden garden.—Have, get, before it cloy,
  Before it cloud, Christ, lord, and sour with sinning,
Innocent mind and Mayday in girl and boy,
  Most, O maid's child, thy choice and worthy the winning.

THE WINDHOVER

To Christ our Lord

I caught this morning morning's minion, king-
dom of daylight's dauphin, dapple-dawn-drawn Falcon, in his riding
Of the rolling level underneath him steady air, and striding
High there, how he rung upon the rein of a wimpling wing
In his ecstasy! then off, off forth on swing,
As a skate's heel sweeps smooth on a bow-bend: the hurl and gliding
Rebuffed the big wind. My heart in hiding
Stirred for a bird,—the achieve of, the mastery of the thing!

Brute beauty and valour and act, oh, air, pride, plume, here
Buckle! AND the fire that breaks from thee then, a billion
Times told lovelier, more dangerous, O my chevalier!
No wonder of it: shéer plód makes plough down sillion
Shine, and blue-bleak embers, ah my dear,
Fall, gall themselves, and gash gold-vermilion.

PIED BEAUTY

Glory be to God for dappled things—
  For skies of couple-colour as a brinded cow;
    For rose-moles all in stipple upon trout that swim;
Fresh-firecoal chestnut-falls; finches' wings;
  Landscape plotted and pieced—fold, fallow, and plough;
    And áll trádes, their gear and tackle and trim.

All things counter, original, spare, strange;
  Whatever is fickle, freckled (who knows how?)
    With swift, slow; sweet, sour; adazzle, dim;
He father's-forth whose beauty is past change:
                                        Praise him.

THOU ART INDEED JUST, LORD

Justus quidem tu es, Domine, si disputem tecum: verumtamen justa loquar ad te: Quare via impiorum prosperatur?

Thou art indeed just, Lord, if I contend
With thee; but, sir, so what I plead is just.
Why do sinners' ways prosper? and why must
Disappointment all I endeavour end?
Wert thou my enemy, O thou my friend,
How wouldst thou worse, I wonder, than thou dost
Defeat, thwart me? Oh, the sots and thralls of lust
Do in spare hours more thrive than I that spend,
Sir, life upon thy cause. See, banks and brakes
Now, leavèd how thick! lacèd they are again
With fretty chervil, look, and fresh wind shakes
Them; birds build—but not I build; no, but strain,
Time's eunuch, and not breed one work that wakes.
Mine, O thou lord of life, send my roots rain.

MY OWN HEART LET ME HAVE MORE PITY ON

My own heart let me have more pity on; let
Me live to my sad self hereafter kind,
Charitable; not live this tormented mind
With this tormented mind tormenting yet.

I cast for comfort I can no more get
By groping round my comfortless, than blind
Eyes in their dark can day or thirst can find
Thirst's all-in-all in all a world of wet.

Soul, self; come, poor Jackself, I do advise
You, jaded, let be; call off thoughts awhile
Elsewhere; leave comfort root-room; let joy size
At God knows when to God knows what; whose smile
's not wrung, see you; unforeseen times rather—as skies
Betweenpie mountains—lights a lovely mile.

I WAKE AND FEEL THE FELL OF DARK

I wake and feel the fell of dark, not day.
What hours, O what black hoürs we have spent
This night! what sights you, heart, saw; ways you went!
And more must, in yet longer light's delay.

With witness I speak this. But where I say
Hours I mean years, mean life. And my lament
Is cries countless, cries like dead letters sent
To dearest him that lives alas! away.

I am gall, I am heartburn. God's most deep decree
Bitter would have me taste: my taste was me;
Bones built in me, flesh filled, blood brimmed the curse.

Selfyeast of spirit a dull dough sours. I see
The lost are like this, and their scourge to be
As I am mine, their sweating selves, but worse.

William Butler Yeats

« 1865 – 1939 »

THE ROSE OF PEACE

If Michael, leader of God's host
When Heaven and Hell are met,
Looked down on you from Heaven's door-post
He would his deeds forget.

Brooding no more upon God's wars
In his divine homestead,
He would go weave out of the stars
A chaplet for your head.

And all folk seeing him bow down,
And white stars tell your praise,
Would come at last to God's great town,
Led on by gentle ways;

And God would bid His warfare cease,
Saying all things were well;
And softly make a rosy peace,
A peace of Heaven with Hell.

TO SOME I HAVE TALKED WITH BY THE FIRE

While I wrought out these fitful Danaan rhymes,
My heart would brim with dreams about the times
When we bent down above the fading coals
And talked of the dark folk who live in souls
Of passionate men, like bats in the dead trees;

And of the wayward twilight companies
Who sigh with mingled sorrow and content,
Because their blossoming dreams have never bent
Under the fruit of evil and of good:
And of the embattled flaming multitude
Who rise, wing above wing, flame above flame,
And, like a storm, cry the Ineffable Name,
And with the clashing of their sword-blades make
A rapturous music, till the morning break
And the white hush end all but the loud beat
Of their long wings, the flash of their white feet.

THE PLAYERS ASK FOR A BLESSING ON THE PSALTERIES AND ON THEMSELVES

Three Voices [*together*]. Hurry to bless the hands that play,
The mouths that speak, the notes and strings,
O masters of the glittering town!
O! lay the shrilly trumpet down,
Though drunken with the flags that sway
Over the ramparts and the towers,
And with the waving of your wings.

First Voice. Maybe they linger by the way.
One gathers up his purple gown;
One leans and mutters by the wall—
He dreads the weight of mortal hours.

Second Voice. O no, O no! they hurry down
Like plovers that have heard the call.

Third Voice. O kinsmen of the Three in One,
O kinsmen, bless the hands that play.
The notes they waken shall live on
When all this heavy history's done;
Our hands, our hands must ebb away.

Three Voices [*together*.] The proud and careless notes live on,
But bless our hands that ebb away.

THE THREE HERMITS

Three old hermits took the air
By a cold and desolate sea,
First was muttering a prayer,
Second rummaged for a flea;
On a windy stone, the third,
Giddy with his hundredth year,
Sang unnoticed like a bird:
'Though the Door of Death is near
And what waits behind the door,
Three times in a single day
I, though upright on the shore,
Fall asleep when I should pray.'
So the first, but now the second:
'We're but given what we have earned
When all thoughts and deeds are reckoned,
So it's plain to be discerned
That the shades of holy men
Who have failed, being weak of will,
Pass the Door of Birth again,
And are plagued by crowds, until
They've the passion to escape.'
Moaned the other, 'They are thrown
Into some most fearful shape.'
But the second mocked his moan:
'They are not changed to anything,
Having loved God once, but maybe
To a poet or a king
Or a witty lovely lady.'
While he'd rummaged rags and hair,
Caught and cracked his flea, the third,
Giddy with his hundredth year,
Sang unnoticed like a bird.

SONG OF A FOOL
(From "Two Songs of a Fool")

A speckled cat and a tame hare
Eat at my hearthstone
And sleep there;
And both look up to me alone
For learning and defence
As I look up to Providence.

I start out of my sleep to think
Some day I may forget
Their food and drink;
Or, the house door left unshut,
The hare may run till it's found
The horn's sweet note and the tooth of the hound.

I bear a burden that might well try
Men that do all by rule,
And what can I
That am a wandering-witted fool
But pray to God that He ease
My great responsibilities?

CRAZY JANE ON GOD

That lover of a night
Came when he would,
Went in the dawning light
Whether I would or no;
Men come, men go,
All things remain in God.

Banners choke the sky;
Men-at-arms tread;

Armoured horses neigh
Where the great battle was
In the narrow pass:
All things remain in God.

Before their eyes a house
That from childhood stood
Uninhabited, ruinous,
Suddenly lit up
From door to top:
All things remain in God.

I had wild Jack for a lover;
Though like a road
That men pass over
My body makes no moan
But sings on:
All things remain in God.

Edwin Arlington Robinson

« 1869 – 1935 »

THE ALTAR

ALONE, remote, nor witting where I went,
I found an altar builded in a dream—
A fiery place, whereof there was a gleam
So swift, so searching, and so eloquent
Of upward promise, that love's murmur, blent
With sorrow's warning, gave but a supreme
Unending impulse to that human stream
Whose flood was all for the flame's fury bent.

Alas! I said,—the world is in the wrong.
But the same quenchless fever of unrest
That thrilled the foremost of that martyred throng
Thrilled me, and I awoke . . . and was the same
Bewildered insect plunging for the flame
That burns, and must burn somehow for the best.

CALVARY

FRIENDLESS and faint, with martyred steps and slow
Faint for the flesh, but for the spirit free,
Stung by the mob that came to see the show,
The Master toiled along to Calvary;
We gibed him, as he went, with houndish glee,
Till his dimmed eyes for us did overflow;
We cursed his vengeless hands thrice wretchedly,—
And this was nineteen hundred years ago.

But after nineteen hundred years the shame
Still clings, and we have not made good the loss
That outraged faith has entered in his name.
Ah, when shall come love's courage to be strong!
Tell me, O Lord—tell me, O Lord, how long
Are we to keep Christ writhing on the cross!

A CHRISTMAS SONNET

For One in Doubt

While you that in your sorrow disavow
Service and hope, see love and brotherhood
Far off as ever, it will do no good
For you to wear his thorns upon your brow
For doubt of him. And should you question how
To serve him best, he might say, if he could,
"Whether or not the cross was made of wood
Whereon you nailed me, is no matter now."

Though other saviors have in older lore
A legend, and for older gods have died—
Though death may wear the crown it always wore
And ignorance be still the sword of pride—
Something was here that was not here before,
And strangely has not yet been crucified.

Robert Frost

« 1874 - 1963 »

TO A YOUNG WRETCH (Boethian)

As gay for you to take your father's ax
As take his gun—rod—to go hunting—fishing.
You nick my spruce until its fiber cracks,
It gives up standing straight and goes down swishing.
You link an arm in its arm and you lean
Across the light snow homeward smelling green.

I could have bought you just as good a tree
To frizzle resin in a candle flame,
And what a saving 'twould have meant to me.
But tree by charity is not the same
As tree by enterprise and expedition.
I must not spoil your Christmas with contrition.

It is your Christmases against my woods.
But even where thus opposing interests kill,
They are to be thought of as opposing goods
Oftener than conflicting good and ill;
Which makes the war god seem no special dunce
For always fighting on both sides at once.

And though in tinsel chain and popcorn rope,
My tree a captive in your window bay
Has lost its footing on my mountain slope
And lost the stars of heaven, may, oh, may
The symbol star it lifts against your ceiling
Help me accept its fate with Christmas feeling.

John Hall Wheelock

« 1886 - »

NIGHT THOUGHTS IN AGE

Light, that out of the west looked back once more
Through lids of cloud, has closed a sleepy eye;
The heaven of stars bends over me its silence,
A harp through which the wind of time still whispers
Music some hand has hushed but left there trembling—
Conceits of an aging man who lies awake
Under familiar rafters, in this leafy
Bird-singing, haunted, green, ancestral spot
Where time has made such music! For often now,
In this belovèd country whose coastal shores
Look seaward, without limit, to the south—
Land of flung spume and spray, sea-winds and -voices,
Where the gull rides the gale on equal wing,
With motionless body and downward-bending head,
Where, in mid-summer days, offshore, the dolphin
Hurdles the water with arching leap and plunge—
I meditate, lying awake, alone,
On the sea's voice and time's receding music,
Felt ebbing in the heart and shrunken vein—
How time, that takes us all, will at the last,
In taking us, take the whole world we are dreaming:
Sun, wind and sea, whisper of rain at night,
The young, hollow-cheeked moon, the clouds of evening
Drifting in a great solitude—all these
Shall time take away, surely, and the face
From which the eyes of love look out at us
In this brief world, this horror-haunted kingdom
Of beauty and of longing and of terror,

Of phantoms and illusion, of appearance
And disappearance—magic of leger-de-main,
Trick of the prestidigitator's wand—
The huge phantasmagoria we are dreaming:
This shall time take from us, and take forever,
When we are taken by that receding music.
O marvel of things, fabulous dream, too soon,
Too soon will the wild blood cry out and death
Quell, with one blow, the inscrutable fantasy!
Shall prayer change this? Youth is the hour for prayer,
That has so much to pray for; a man's life,
Lived howsoever, is a long reconcilement
To the high, lonely, unforgiving truth,
Which will not change for his or any prayer,
Now or hereafter: in that reconcilement
Lies all of wisdom. Age is the hour for praise,
Praise that is joy, praise that is acquiescence,
Praise that is adoration and gratitude
For all that has been given and not been given.
Night flows on. The wind, that all night through
Quickened the treetops with a breath of ocean,
Veers inland, falls away, and the sea's voice,
Learned in lost childhood, a remembered music,
By day or night, through love, through sleep, through dream,
Still breathing its perpetual benediction,
Has dwindled to a sigh. By the west window,
In the soft dark the leaves of the sycamore
Stir gently, rustle, and are still, are listening
To a silence that is music. The old house
Is full of ghosts, dear ghosts on stair and landing,
Ghosts in chamber and hall; garden and walk
Are marvellous with ghosts, where so much love
Dwelt for a little while and made such music,
Before it too was taken by the tide
That takes us all, of time's receding music.
Oh, all is music! All has been turned to music!
All that is vanished has been turned to music!
And these familiar rafters, that have known
The child, the young man and the man, now shelter
The aging man who lies here, listening, listening—
All night, in a half dream, I have lain here listening.

Edwin Muir

« 1887 - 1959 »

THE DAY

If, in the mind of God or book of fate,
This day that's all to live lies lived and done,
And there already like Griseldas wait
My apprentice thoughts and actions, still untried;
If, where I travel, some thing or some one
Has gone before me sounding through the wide
Immensity of nothingness to make
A region and a road where road was none,
Nor shape, nor shaping hand; if for my sake
The elected joy grows there and the chosen pain
In the field of good and ill, in surety sown:
Oh give me clarity and love that now
The way I walk may truly trace again
The in eternity written and hidden way;
Make pure my heart and will, and me allow
The acceptance and revolt, the yea and nay,
The denial and the blessing that are my own.

THE SON

This hungry flesh and bone
That white and black and brown
Share was shared by One
Once who to death went down.

Son of God and of Man,
He breathed as ours his breath,
And in this body ran
The crooked road to death.

Night and day and night
Wheeled him through time and space,
Whose hour was changeless light,
Infinity his place.

Time's essential heat
Bound him inside the womb
And in his arteries beat
The proud march to the tomb.

He from eternity
Stared now through a little eye,
That God and Man might see
The good and the wicked die.

Born, his babbling tongue
Told infancy's helplessness,
Disgrace of being young,
Adolescent distress,

Till manhood's brutal force
Through all his veins rolled on
Wild as a headstrong horse,
Though he was Heaven's son.

Thirst like a rusty knife,
Dry hunger he withstood,
Who had the water of life
And the immortal food.

The skill of the carpenter,
The sailor's dauntless heart
He learned, lest he should mar,
A God, his second part.

Happiness not of Heaven,
And unimmortal sorrows
He chose, talk in the evening,
And the wild mounting morrows

That wound in narrowing rings
Up to the waiting Tree
Through treachery of things
And men's treachery.

Till only despair was left;
'Me why hast Thou forsaken?'
God of God bereft
Down from the tree was taken,

That so the Light shine through
The first to the last pain,
And all be made new
Down to the last grain.

Ordinary men
Saw him take his fall.
All is changed since then;
He is joined with all.

T. S. Eliot

« 1888 – »

CHORUSES FROM "THE ROCK"

– IX –

Son of Man, behold with thine eyes, and hear with thine ears
And set thine heart upon all that I show thee.
Who is this that has said: the House of GOD is a House of Sorrow;
We must walk in black and go sadly, with long-drawn faces,
We must go between empty walls, quavering lowly, whispering faintly,
Among a few flickering scattered lights?
They would put upon GOD their own sorrow, the grief they should feel
For their sins and faults as they go about their daily occasions.
Yet they walk in the street proudnecked, like thoroughbreds ready for races,
Adorning themselves, and busy in the market, the forum,
And all other secular meetings.
Thinking good of themselves, ready for any festivity,
Doing themselves very well.
Let us mourn in a private chamber, learning the way of penitence,
And then let us learn the joyful communion of saints.

The soul of Man must quicken to creation.
Out of the formless stone, when the artist united himself with stone,
Spring always new forms of life, from the soul of man that is joined to the soul of stone;
Out of the meaningless practical shapes of all that is living or lifeless
Joined with the artist's eye, new life, new form, new colour.
Out of the sea of sound the life of music,
Out of the slimy mud of words, out of the sleet and hail of verbal imprecisions,
Approximate thoughts and feelings, words that have taken the place of thoughts and feelings,
There spring the perfect order of speech, and the beauty of incantation.

LORD, shall we not bring these gifts to Your service?
Shall we not bring to Your service all our powers
For life, for dignity, grace and order,
And intellectual pleasures of the senses?
The LORD who created must wish us to create
And employ our creation again in His service
Which is already His service in creating.
For Man is joined spirit and body,
And therefore must serve as spirit and body.
Visible and invisible, two worlds meet in Man;
Visible and invisible must meet in His temple;
You must not deny the body.

Now you shall see the Temple completed:
After much striving, after many obstacles;
For the work of creation is never without travail;
The formed stone, the visible crucifix,
The dressed altar, the lifting light,

Light

Light
The visible reminder of Invisible Light.

– X –

You have seen the house built, you have seen it adorned
By one who came in the night, it is now dedicated to GOD.
It is now a visible church, one more light set on a hill
In a world confused and dark and disturbed by portents of fear.
And what shall we say of the future? Is one church all we can build?
Or shall the Visible Church go on to conquer the World?

The great snake lies ever half awake, at the bottom of the pit of the world, curled
In folds of himself until he awakens in hunger and moving his head to right and to left prepares for his hour to devour.
But the Mystery of Iniquity is a pit too deep for mortal eyes to plumb. Come
Ye out from among those who prize the serpent's golden eyes,
The worshippers, self-given sacrifice of the snake. Take
Your way and be ye separate.
Be not too curious of Good and Evil;

Seek not to count the future waves of Time;
But be ye satisfied that you have light
Enough to take your step and find your foothold.

O Light Invisible, we praise Thee!
Too bright for mortal vision.
O Greater Light, we praise Thee for the less;
The eastern light our spires touch at morning,
The light that slants upon our western doors at evening,
The twilight over stagnant pools at batflight,
Moon light and star light, owl and moth light,
Glow-worm glowlight on a grassblade.
O Light Invisible, we worship Thee!

We thank Thee for the lights that we have kindled,
The light of altar and of sanctuary;
Small lights of those who meditate at midnight
And lights directed through the coloured panes of windows
And light reflected from the polished stone,
The gilded carven wood, the coloured fresco.
Our gaze is submarine, our eyes look upward
And see the light that fractures through unquiet water.
We see the light but see not whence it comes.
O Light Invisible, we glorify Thee!

In our rhythm of earthly life we tire of light. We are glad when the day ends, when the play ends; and ecstasy is too much pain.
We are children quickly tired: children who are up in the night and fall asleep as the rocket is fired; and the day is long for work or play.
We tire of distraction or concentration, we sleep and are glad to sleep,
Controlled by the rhythm of blood and the day and the night and the seasons.
And we must extinguish the candle, put out the light and relight it;
Forever must quench, forever relight the flame.
Therefore we thank Thee for our little light, that is dappled with shadow.
We thank Thee who has moved us to building, to finding, to forming at the ends of our fingers and beams of our eyes.
And when we have built an altar to the Invisible Light, we may set thereon the little lights for which our bodily vision is made.
And we thank Thee that darkness reminds us of light.
O Light Invisible, we give Thee thanks for Thy great glory!

Memnon

Tithonus, the husband of Aurora, the Goddess of the Dawn, was the father of her son, the dark-skinned prince Memnon of Ethiopia was killed at Troy fighting for the Trojans.

A great statue was erected in Egypt at Thebes to him, and it was said that when the first rays of the dawn fell upon it a sound came from it like the twanging of a harpstring.

Chekhov?

Conrad Aiken

« 1889 – »

PRELUDES FOR MEMNON

– III –

Sleep: and between the closed eyelids of sleep,
From the dark spirit's still unresting grief,
The one tear burns its way. O God, O God,
What monstrous world is this, whence no escape
Even in sleep? Between the fast-shut lids
This one tear comes, hangs on the lashes, falls:
Symbol of some gigantic dream, that shakes
The secret-sleeping soul. . . . And I descend
By a green cliff that fronts the worldlong sea;
Disastrous shore; where bones of ships and rocks
Are mixed; and beating waves bring in the sails
Of unskilled mariners, ill-starred. The gulls
Fall in a cloud upon foul flotsam there;
The air resounds with cries of scavengers.

Dream: and between the close-locked lids of dream
The terrible infinite intrudes its blue:
Ice: silence: death: the abyss of Nothing.
O God, O God, let the sore soul have peace.
Deliver it from this bondage of harsh dreams.
Release this shadow from its object, this object
From its shadow. Let the fleet soul go nimbly,—
Down,—Down,—from step to step of dark,—
From dark to deeper dark, from dark to rest.
And let no Theseus-thread of memory
Shine in that labyrinth, or on those stairs,
To guide her back; nor bring her, where she lies,
Remembrance of a torn world well forgot.

e. e. cummings

« 1894 – 1962 »

WHEN GOD LETS MY BODY BE

when god lets my body be

From each brave eye shall sprout a tree
fruit that dangles therefrom

the purpled world will dance upon
Between my lips which did sing

a rose shall beget the spring
that maidens whom passion wastes

will lay between their little breasts
My strong fingers beneath the snow

Into strenuous birds shall go
my love walking in the grass

their wings will touch with her face
and all the while shall my heart be

With the bulge and nuzzle of the sea

I THANK YOU GOD FOR MOST THIS AMAZING

i thank You God for most this amazing
day:for the leaping greenly spirits of trees
and a blue true dream of sky;and for everything
which is natural which is infinite which is yes

(i who have died am alive again today,
and this is the sun's birthday;this is the birth
day of life and of love and wings:and of the gay
great happening illimitably earth)

how should tasting touching hearing seeing
breathing any—lifted from the no
of all nothing—human merely being
doubt unimaginable You?

(now the ears of my ears awake and
now the eyes of my eyes are opened)

IN TIME OF DAFFODILS

in time of daffodils(who know
the goal of living is to grow)
forgetting why,remember how

in time of lilacs who proclaim
the aim of waking is to dream,
remember so(forgetting seem)

in time of roses(who amaze
our now and here with paradise)
forgetting if, remember yes

in time of all sweet things beyond
whatever mind may comprehend,
remember seek(forgetting find)

and in a mystery to be
(when time from time shall set us free)
forgetting me,remember me

FROM SPIRALLING ECSTATICALLY THIS

from spiralling ecstatically this

proud nowhere of earth's most prodigious night
blossoms a newborn babe:around him,eyes
—gifted with every keener appetite
than mere unmiracle can quite appease—
humbly in their imagined bodies kneel
(over time space doom dream while floats the whole

perhapsless mystery of paradise)

mind without soul may blast some universe
to might have been,and stop ten thousand stars
but not one heartbeat of this child;nor shall
even prevail a million questionings
against the silence of his mother's smile

—whose only secret all creation sings

Hart Crane

« 1899 – 1932 »

AVE MARIA (from "The Bridge")

Venient annis sæcula seris,
Quibus Oceanus vincula rerum
Laxet et ingens pateat tellus
Tethysque novos detegat orbes
Nec sit terris ultima Thule.—SENECA

Columbus, alone, gazing toward Spain, invokes the presence of two faithful partisans of his quest . . .

Be with me, Luis de San Angel, now—
Witness before the tides can wrest away
The word I bring, O you who reined my suit
Into the Queen's great heart that doubtful day;
For I have seen now what no perjured breath
Of clown nor sage can riddle or gainsay:—
To you, too, Juan Perez, whose counsel fear
And greed adjourned,—I bring you back Cathay!

Here waves climb into dusk on gleaming mail;
Invisible valves of the sea,—locks, tendons
Crested and creeping, troughing corridors
That fall back yawning to another plunge.
Slowly the sun's red caravel drops light
Once more behind us. . . . It is morning there—
O where our Indian emperies lie revealed,
Yet lost, all, let this keel one instant yield!

I thought of Genoa; and this truth, now proved,
That made me exile in her streets, stood me
More absolute than ever—biding the moon
Till dawn should clear that dim frontier, first seen
—The Chan's great continent. . . . Then faith, not fear

Nigh surged me witless. . . . Hearing the surf near—
I, wonder-breathing, kept the watch,—saw
The first palm chevron the first lighted hill.

And lowered. And they came out to us crying,
"The Great White Birds!" (O Madre Maria, still
One ship of these thou grantest safe returning;
Assure us through thy mantle's ageless blue!)
And record of more, floating in a cask,
Was tumbled from us under bare poles scudding;
And later hurricanes may claim more pawn. . . .
For here between two worlds, another, harsh,

This third, of water, tests the word; lo, here
Bewilderment and mutiny heap whelming
Laughter, and shadow cuts sleep from the heart
Almost as though the Moor's flung scimitar
Found more than flesh to fathom in its fall.
Yet under tempest-lash and surfeitings
Some inmost sob, half-heard, dissuades the abyss,
Merges the wind in measure to the waves,

Series on series, infinite,—till eyes
Starved wide on blackened tides, accrete—enclose
This turning rondure whole, this crescent ring
Sun-cusped and zoned with modulated fire
Like pearls that whisper through the Doge's hands
—Yet no delirium of jewels! O Fernando,
Take of that eastern shore, this western sea,
Yet yield thy God's, thy Virgin's charity!
—Rush down the plenitude, and you shall see
Isaiah counting famine on this lee!

*

An herb, a stray branch among salty teeth,
The jellied weeds that drag the shore,—perhaps
Tomorrow's moon will grant us Saltes Bar—
Palos again,—a land cleared of long war.
Some Angelus environs the cordage tree;
Dark waters onward shake the dark prow free.

*

O Thou who sleepest on Thyself, apart
Like ocean athwart lanes of death and birth,
And all the eddying breath between dost search
Cruelly with love thy parable of man,—
Inquisitor! incognizable Word
Of Eden and the enchained Sepulchre,
Into thy steep savannahs, burning blue,
Utter to loneliness the sail is true.

Who grindest oar, and arguing the mast
Subscribest holocaut of ships, O Thou
Within whose primal scan consummately
The glistening seignories of Ganges swim;—
Who sendest greeting by the corposant,
And Teneriffe's garnet—flamed it in a cloud,
Urging through night our passage to the Chan;—
Te Deum laudamus, for thy teeming span!

Of all that amplitude that time explores,
A needle in the sight, suspended north,—
Yielding by inference and discard, faith
And true appointment from the hidden shoal:
This disposition that thy night relates
From Moon to Saturn in one sapphire wheel:
The orbic wake of thy once whirling feet,
Elohim, still I hear thy sounding heel!

White toil of heaven's cordons, mustering
In holy rings all sails charged to the far
Hushed gleaming fields and pendant seething wheat
Of knowledge,—round thy brows unhooded now
—The kindled Crown! acceded of the poles
And biassed by full sails, meridians reel
Thy purpose—still one shore beyond desire!
The sea's green crying towers a-sway, Beyond

And kingdoms
naked in the
trembling heart—
Te Deum laudamus
O Thou Hand of Fire

C. Day Lewis

« 1904 – »

TEMPT ME NO MORE

Tempt me no more; for I
Have known the lightning's hour,
The poet's inward pride,
The certainty of power.

Bayonets are closing round.
I shrink; yet I must wring
A living from despair
And out of steel a song.

Though song, though breath be short,
I'll share not the disgrace
Of those that ran away
Or never left the base.

Comrades, my tongue can speak
No comfortable words;
Calls to a forlorn hope
Give work and not rewards.

Oh keep the sickle sharp
And follow still the plow:
Others may reap, though some
See not the winter through.

Father who endest all,
Pity our broken sleep;
For we lie down with tears
And waken but to weep.

And if our blood alone
Will melt this iron earth,
Take it. It is well spent
Easing a savior's birth.

Richard Eberhart

« 1904 – »

THE BOOK OF NATURE

(UNDERCLIFF, 1952)

As I was reading the book of nature
In the fall of the year
And picking the full blueberries
Each as round as a tear;

As I was being in my boyhood
Scanning the book of the rocks,
Intercepting the wrath to come
Where the hay was in the shocks;

As I was eye-drinking the waters
As they came up Seal Cove
With the eyes of my dazzled daughter
An absolutist of a sudden grove;

As I was on that sea again
With islands stretching off the sail,
The real sea of mysterious time,
Islands of summer storm and hail;

As I was living with the love of death,
A concentrated wonder of the birches,
Passionate in the shudder of the air
And running on the splendour of the waters;

As I was a person in the sea birds,
And I was a spirit of the ferns,

And I was a dream of the monadnocks,
An intelligence of the flocks and herds;

As I was a memory of memory,
Keeper of the holy seals,
The unified semblance of disparates
And wielder of the real;

As I was happy as the ospreys,
As I was full of broom and bright afflatus,
As I was a vehicle of silence
Being the sound of a sudden hiatus;

As I was the purified exemplar
And sufferer of the whole adventure,
And as I was desire in despair,
A bird's eye in doom's nature;

As I stood in the whole, immaculate air,
Holding all things together,
I was blessed in the knowledge of nature.
God is man's weather.

Then I saw God on my fingertip
And I was glad for all who ever lived,
Serene and exalted in mood,
Whatever the mind contrived.

Then God provided an answer
Out of the overwhelming skies and years
And wrath and judgment then and there
Shook out the human tears.

Robert Penn Warren

« 1905 – »

SUMMER STORM (*circa* 1916), AND GOD'S GRACE

Toward sun, the sun flared suddenly red.
  The green of woods was doused to black.
  The cattle bellowed by the haystack.
Redder than ever, red clay was red.
  Up the lane the plowhands came pelting back.

Astride and no saddle, and they didn't care
  If a razor-back mule at a break-tooth trot
  Was not the best comfort a man ever got,
But came huddling on, with jangling gear,
  And the hat that jounced off stayed off, like as not.

In that strange light all distance died.
  You know the world's intensity.
  Field-far, you can read the aphid's eye.
The mole, in his sod, can no more hide,
  And weeps beneath the naked sky.

Past silence, sound insinuates
  Past ear into the inner brain.
  The toad's asthmatic breath is pain,
The cutworm's tooth grinds and grates,
  And the root, in earth, screams, screams again,

But no cloud yet. No wind, though you,
  A half a county off, now spy
  The crow that, laboring zenith-high,
Is suddenly, with wings askew,
  Snatched, and tumbled down the sky.

And so you waited. You couldn't talk.
  The creek-side willows shuddered gray.
  The oak leaf turned the other way,
Gray as fish-belly. Then, with a squawk,
  The henhouse heaved, and flew away,

And darkness rode in on the wind.
  The pitchfork lightning tossed the trees,
  And God got down on hands and knees
To peer and cackle and commend
  His own sadistic idiocies.

Next morning you stood where the bridge had washed out.
  A drowned cow bobbled down the creek.
  Raw-eyed, men watched. They did not speak.
Till one shrugged, said he thought he'd make out.
  Then turned, took the woods-path up the creek

Oh, send them summer, one summer just right,
  With rain well spaced, no wind or hail.
  Let cutworm tooth falter, locust jaw fail,
And if a man wake at roof-roar at night,
  Let that roar be the roar of God's awful Grace,
  And not of His flail.

W. H. Auden

« 1907 – »

PETITION

Sir, no man's enemy, forgiving all
But will its negative inversion, be prodigal:
Send to us power and light, a sovereign touch
Curing the intolerable neural itch,
The exhaustion of weaning, the liar's quinsy,
And the distortions of ingrown virginity.
Prohibit sharply the rehearsed response
And gradually correct the coward's stance;
Cover in time with beams those in retreat
That, spotted, they turn though the reverse were great;
Publish each healer that in city lives
Or country houses at the end of drives;
Harrow the house of the dead; look shining at
New styles of architecture, a change of heart.

Theodore Roethke

« 1908 – 1963 »

THE VIGIL (from "Four for Sir John Davies")

Dante attained the purgatorial hill,
Trembled at hidden virtue without flaw,
Shook with a mighty power beyond his will,—
Did Beatrice deny what Dante saw?
All lovers live by longing, and endure:
Summon a vision and declare it pure.

Though everything's astonishment at last,
Who leaps to heaven at a single bound?
The links were soft between us; still, we kissed;
We undid chaos to a curious sound:
The waves broke easy, cried to me in white;
Her look was morning in the dying light.

The visible obscures. But who knows when?
Things have their thought: they are the shards of me;
I thought that once, and thought comes round again;
Rapt, we leaned forth with what we could not see.
We danced to shining; mocked before the black
And shapeless night that made no answer back.

The world is for the living. Who are they?
We dared the dark to reach the white and warm.
She was the wind when wind was in my way;
Alive at noon, I perished in her form.
Who rise from flesh to spirit know the fall:
The word outleaps the world, and light is all.

A WALK IN LATE SUMMER

– 1 –

A gull rides on the ripples of a dream,
White upon white, slow-settling on a stone;
Across my lawn the soft-backed creatures come;
In the weak light they wander, each alone.
Bring me the meek, for I would know their ways;
I am a connoisseur of midnight eyes.
The small! The small! I hear them singing clear
On the long banks, in the soft summer air.

– 2 –

What is there for the soul to understand?
The slack face of the dismal pure inane?
The wind dies down; my will dies with the wind,
God's in that stone, or I am not a man!
Body and soul transcend appearances
Before the caving-in of all that is;
I'm dying piecemeal, fervent in decay;
My moments linger—that's eternity.

– 3 –

A late rose ravages the casual eye,
A blaze of being on a central stem.
It lies upon us to undo the lie
Of living merely in the realm of time.
Existence moves toward a certain end—
A thing all earthly lovers understand.
That dove's elaborate way of coming near
Reminds me I am dying with the year.

– 4 –

A tree arises on a central plain—
It is no trick of change or chance of light.
A tree all out of shape from wind and rain,
A tree thinned by the wind obscures my sight.

The long day dies; I walk the woods alone;
Beyond the ridge two wood thrush sing as one.
Being delights in being, and in time.
The evening wraps me, steady as a flame.

THE EXULTING (from "The Dying Man")

Once I delighted in a single tree;
The loose air sent me running like a child—
I love the world; I want more than the world,
Or after-image of the inner eye.
Flesh cries to flesh; and bone cries out to bone;
I die into this life, alone yet not alone.

Was it a god his suffering renewed?—
I saw my father shrinking in his skin;
He turned his face: there was another man,
Walking the edge, loquacious, unafraid.
He quivered like a bird in birdless air,
Yet dared to fix his vision anywhere.

Fish feed on fish, according to their need:
My enemies renew me, and my blood
Beats slower in my careless solitude.
I bare a wound, and dare myself to bleed.
I think a bird, and it begins to fly.
By dying daily, I have come to be.

All exultation is a dangerous thing.
I see you, love, I see you in a dream;
I hear a noise of bees, a trellis hum,
And that slow humming rises into song.
A breath is but a breath: I have the earth;
I shall undo all dying by my death.

THEY SING, THEY SING (from "The Dying Man")

All women love dance in a dying light—
The moon's my mother: how I love the moon!
Out of her place she comes, a dolphin one,
Then settles back to shade and the long night.
A beast cries out as if its flesh were torn,
And that cry takes me back where I was born.

Who thought love but a motion in the mind?
Am I but nothing, leaning towards a thing?
I'll scare myself with sighing, or I'll sing;
Descend, O gentlest light, descend, descend.
O sweet field far ahead, I hear your birds,
They sing, they sing, but still in minor thirds.

I've the lark's word for it, who sings alone:
What's seen recedes; Forever's what we know!—
Eternity defined, and strewn with straw,
The fury of the slug beneath the stone.
The vision moves, and yet remains the same.
In heaven's praise, I dread the thing I am.

The edges of the summit still appal
When we brood on the dead or the beloved;
Nor can imagination do it all
In this last place of light: he dares to live
Who stops being a bird, yet beats his wings
Against the immense immeasurable emptiness of things.

Dylan Thomas

« 1914 – 1953 »

CEREMONY AFTER A FIRE RAID

– I –

Myselves
The grievers
Grieve
Among the street burned to tireless death
A child of a few hours
With its kneading mouth
Charred on the black breast of the grave
The mother dug, and its arms full of fires.

Begin
With singing
Sing
Darkness kindled back into beginning
When the caught tongue nodded blind,
A star was broken
Into the centuries of the child
Myselves grieve now, and miracles cannot atone.

Forgive
Us Forgive
Us your death that myselves the believers
May hold it in a great flood
Till the blood shall spurt,
And the dust shall sing like a bird
As the grains blow, as your death grows,
  through our heart.

Crying
Your dying
Cry,
Child beyond cockcrow, by the fire-dwarfed
Street we chant the flying sea
In the body bereft.
Love is the last light spoken. Oh
Seed of sons in the loin of the black husk left.

– II –

I know not whether
Adam or Eve, the adorned holy bullock
Or the white ewe lamb
Or the chosen virgin
Laid in her snow
On the altar of London,
Was the first to die
In the cinder of the little skull,
O bride and bride groom
O Adam and Eve together
Lying in the lull
Under the sad breast of the head stone
White as the skeleton
Of the garden of Eden.
I know the legend
Of Adam and Eve is never for a second
Silent in my service
Over the dead infants
Over the one
Child who was priest and servants,
Word, singers, and tongue
In the cinder of the little skull,
Who was the serpent's
Nightfall and the fruit like a sun,
Man and woman undone,
Beginning crumbled back to darkness
Bare as the nurseries
Of the garden of wilderness.

– III –

Into the organpipes and steeples
Of the luminous cathedrals,
Into the weathercocks' molten mouths
Rippling into twelve-winded circles,
Into the dead clock burning the hour
Over the urn of sabbaths
Over the whirling ditch of daybreak
Over the sun's hovel and the slum of fire
And the golden pavements laid in requiems,
Into the bread in a wheatfield of flames,
Into the wine burning like brandy,
The masses of the sea
The masses of the sea under
The masses of the infant-bearing sea
Erupt, fountain, and enter to utter for ever
Glory glory glory
The sundering ultimate kingdom of genesis'
  thunder.

AND DEATH SHALL HAVE NO DOMINION

And death shall have no dominion.
Dead men naked they shall be one
With the man in the wind and the west moon;
When their bones are picked clean and the clean bones gone,
They shall have stars at elbow and foot;
Though they go mad they shall be sane,
Though they sink through the sea they shall rise again;
Though lovers be lost love shall not;
And death shall have no dominion.

And death shall have no dominion.
Under the windings of the sea
They lying long shall not die windily;
Twisting on racks when sinews give way,
Strapped to a wheel, yet they shall not break;

Faith in their hands shall snap in two,
And the unicorn evils run them through;
Split all ends up they shan't crack;
And death shall have no dominion.

And death shall have no dominion.
No more may gulls cry at their ears
Or waves break loud on the seashores;
Where blew a flower may a flower no more
Lift its head to the blows of the rain;
Though they be mad and dead as nails,
Heads of the characters hammer through daisies;
Break in the sun till the sun breaks down,
And death shall have no dominion.

John Ciardi

« 1916 – »

AUNT MARY

Aunt Mary died of eating twelve red peppers
after a hard day's work. The doctor said
it was her high blood pressure finished her.
As if disease were anything to Aunt Mary
who had all of her habits to die of! But imagine
a last supper of twelve red peppers, twelve
of those crab-apple size dry scorchers
you buy on a string at Italian groceries,
twelve of them fried in oil and gobbled off
(Aunt Mary was a messy eater)—and then,
to feel the room go dizzy, and through your blood
the awful coming on of nothing more
than twelve red peppers you know you shouldn't have eaten
but couldn't help yourself, they were so good.

Now what shall I pray for gluttonous Aunt Mary
who loved us till we screamed? Even poor Mother
had more of Aunt Mary's love than she could live with,
but had to live with it. I am talking now
of a house with people in it, every room
a life of a sort, a clutter of its own.
I am talking of a scene in the palm of God
in which one actor dies of twelve red peppers,
one has too many children, one a boy friend,
two are out of work, and one is yowling
for one (offstage) to open the bathroom door.
This is not the scene from the palm of God
in which the actors hold God in their palms,
nor the scene in which the actors know their prayers—

it is the scene in which Aunt Mary died
  and nobody knew anything, least of all
  Aunt Mary. In her red-hot transformation
  from gluttony into embalmer's calm
  and candlelight, I cried a hypocrite tear.
  But it was there, when I had seen Aunt Mary
  Bloodlet for God, that I began to see
  what scene we are. At once I wept Aunt Mary
  with a real tear, forgiving all her love,
  and its stupidities, in the palm of God.
  Or on a ledge of time. Or in the eye
  of the blasting sun. Or tightroped on a theorem.
  —Let every man select his own persuasion:
  I pray the tear she taught me of us all.

Robert Lowell

« 1917 – »

COLLOQUY IN BLACK ROCK

Here the jack-hammer jabs into the ocean;
My heart, your race and stagger and demand
More blood-gangs for your nigger-brass percussions,
Till I, the stunned machine of your devotion,
Clanging upon this cymbal of a hand,
Am rattled screw and footloose. All discussions

End in the mud-flat detritus of death.
My heart, beat faster, faster. In Black Mud
Hungarian workmen give their blood
For the martyre Stephen, who was stoned to death.

Black Mud, a name to conjure with: O mud
For watermelons gutted to the crust,
Mud for the mole-tide harbor, mud for mouse,
Mud for the armored Diesel fishing tubs that thud
A year and a day to wind and tide; the dust
Is on this skipping heart that shakes my house,

House of our Savior who was hanged till death.
My heart, beat faster, faster. In Black Mud
Stephen the martyre was broken down to blood:
Our ransom is the rubble of his death.

Christ walks on the black water. In Black Mud
Darts the kingfisher. On Corpus Christi, heart,
Over the drum-beat of St. Stephen's choir
I hear him, *Stupor Mundi,* and the mud
Flies from his hunching wings and beak—my heart,
The blue kingfisher dives on you in fire.

Richard Wilbur

« 1921 – »

LOVE CALLS US TO THE THINGS OF THIS WORLD

The eyes open to a cry of pulleys,
And spirited from sleep, the astounded soul
Hangs for a moment bodiless and simple
As false dawn.
Outside the open window
The morning air is all awash with angels.

Some are in bed-sheets, some are in blouses,
Some are in smocks: but truly there they are.
Now they are rising together in calm swells
Of halcyon feeling, filling whatever they wear
With the deep joy of their impersonal breathing;

Now they are flying in place, conveying
The terrible speed of their omnipresence, moving
And staying like white water; and now of a sudden
They swoon down into so rapt a quiet
That nobody seems to be there.
The soul shrinks

From all that it is about to remember,
From the punctual rape of every blessèd day,
And cries,
"Oh, let there be nothing on earth but laundry,
Nothing but rosy hands in the rising steam
And clear dances done in the sight of heaven."

Yet, as the sun acknowledges
With a warm look the world's hunks and colors,

The soul descends once more in bitter love
To accept the waking body, saying now
In a changed voice as the man yawns and rises,

"Bring them down from their ruddy gallows;
Let there be clean linen for the backs of thieves;
Let lovers go fresh and sweet to be undone,
And the heaviest nuns walk in a pure floating
Of dark habits,
keeping their difficult balance."

Vassar Miller

« 1924 – »

THE TREE OF SILENCE

Upon the branches of our silence hang our words,
Half-ripened fruit.
Gone are the months of summer, gone
Beyond pursuit.
Let us leave, though pinched and wan,
The windfalls wither
Under the tree whose shade affords
No shelter either.

For when was language ever food for human yearning!
Sun-gilded rain
Mocking the sheen of golden peach,
Words only drain
Hearts of strength; let mortal speech
Make time and way
For life, the long and lonely learning
How to pray.

FANTASY ON THE RESURRECTION

Flaws cling to flesh as dews cling to a rose:
The cripples limp as though they would prolong,
Walking, a waltz; the deaf ears, opened, close
As if their convolutions hoard all song;
The blind eyes keep half shut as if to fold
A vision fast men never glimpse by staring;

Against their will the mute lips move that hold
A language which was never tongue's for sharing.
Shocked shag of earth and everything thereunder
Turned inside out—the nail-gnarled have caught Heaven
Like a bright ball. Not in their reknit wonder,
But in their wounds lies Christ's sprung grace engraven—
Not in the body lighter than word spoken,
But in the side still breached, the hands still broken.

W. S. Merwin

« 1927 – »

THE ISAIAH OF SOUILLAC

Why the prophet is dancing the sculptor knew. If
The prophet is dancing. Or even if it is only
Wind, a wind risen there in the doorway
Suddenly as a fish leaps, lifting his garments
His feet, like music, a whirling of breath carved
There in the narrow place that is enough for a man.
You see a wind in its signs but in itself not.
You hear a spirit in its motion, in its words, even
In its stillness, but in itself not. Know it here in the stance
Of a prophet, and his beard blown in a doorway.
His words stream in the stoney wind; woe
Unto the dust that is deaf, for even stones
Can rise as with feet when the spirit passes
Upon the place where they are. But they are all gone away
Backward; from the soles of their feet to their heedless heads
There is no measure nor soundness in them. His fingers,
Frail as reeds making the music they move to,
Embody a lightness like fire. They shall be moved
With burning whom this breath moves not, who have refused
The waters of Shiloah that go softly shall the river
Rise over, out in the sunlight, roaring
Like the sea, like lions, spreading its wings like a wind.
And yet will the wind of heaven wear the shape of a man,
Be mortal as breath, before men, for a sign, and stand
Between good and evil, the thieves of the left and right hand.
And the sign of a wind is dancing, the motion
Of a sign is dancing and ushered with words beating
And with dancing. So there is terrible gentleness
Unleashed in the stone of his eyes, so

The words dance as a fire, as a clapping
Of hands, as the stars dance, as the mountains
Leap swelling, as the feet of the prophet, faithful
Upon them, dance, dance, and still to the same song.

MARINERS' CAROL

So still the night swinging,
Wind of our faring,
Only the bows' seethe to lap us,
Stays and wake whispering,
The thin bell striking,
And our hearts in their blindness.
O star, shine before us!

The serpent's deep sliding,
Wind of our faring,
Is everywhere around us,
Heaves under us, gliding;
We know its toothed curling
The whole world encircles.
O star, shine before us!

Crushed in its drag and keeping,
Wind of our faring,
The darkened dead have no peace,
World-without-end shifting;
All, all are there, and no resting.
It exults above their faces.
O star, shine before us!

The horizon's perfect ring,
Wind of our faring,
None enters nor ever has.
And we, like a cradle, rocking:
For the first glimpse of our homing
We roll and are restless.
O star, shine before us!

Till, heaven and earth joining,
Wind of our faring,
It is born to us
Like the first line of dawn breaking;
For that word and sight yearning
We keep the long watches.
O star, shine before us!

Ted Hughes

« 1930 – »

THE MARTYRDOM OF BISHOP FARRAR

Burned by Bloody Mary's men at Caermarthen. "If I flinch from the pain of the burning, believe not the doctrine that I have preached." (His words on being chained to the stake.)

Bloody Mary's venomous flames can curl;
They can shrivel sinew and char bone
Of foot, ankle, knee, and thigh, and boil
Bowels, and drop his heart a cinder down;
And her soldiers can cry, as they hurl
Logs in the red rush: "This is her sermon."

The sullen-jowled watching Welsh townspeople
Hear him crack in the fire's mouth; they see what
Black oozing twist of stuff bubbles the smell
That tars and retches their lungs: no pulpit
Of his ever held their eyes so still,
Never, as now his agony, his wit.

An ignorant means to establish ownership
Of his flock! Thus their shepherd she seized
And knotted him into this blazing shape
In their eyes, as if such could have cauterized
The trust they turned towards him, and branded on
Its stump her claim, to outlaw question.

So it might have been: seeing their exemplar
And teacher burned for his lessons to black bits,
Their silence might have disowned him to her,
And hung up what he had taught with their Welsh hats:
Who sees his blasphemous father struck by fire
From heaven, might well be heard to speak no oaths.

But the fire that struck here, come from Hell even,
Kindled little heavens in his words
As he fed his body to the flame alive.
Words which, before they will be dumbly spared,
Will burn their body and be tongued with fire
Make paltry folly of flesh and this world's air.

When they saw what annuities of hours
And comfortable blood he burned to get
His words a bare honouring in their ears,
The shrewd townsfolk pocketed them hot:
Stamp was not current but they rang and shone
As good gold as any queen's crown.

Gave all he had, and yet the bargain struck
To a merest farthing his whole agony,
His body's cold-kept miserdom of shrieks
He gave uncounted, while out of his eyes,
Out of his mouth, fire like a glory broke,
And smoke burned his sermons into the skies.

Jon Silkin

« 1930 – »

TO COME OUT SINGING

– I –

I came out singing
And the song was a cry into the green world.
Easily I came into this world.
Then why should it cry? And for whom?
Not for you smoke of ghost, dead chosen people,
Not for you invisible murderers, I did not spring
Out like a cry singing for you. I came
Out of God's six winged folded desert
Because there was promised me one love.
But out of that promise
From that cry, two worlds sprang
Entire, perfect.
The cry is, I tell you, for one of these.
Yet its promise comes and comes bearing a double fruit
A treble cry a green song
A crying green tree a terrible word.
A terrible fruit has opened its division
A fair fruit terrible in division.

– II –

But who has promised?
A new being bridles in the present.
And that is a promise.
But who has said to you love?
The god inside me promised me
Spoke you the word.

But I delivered the promise
I cried love.
Also I broke the bread
I kindled fire.
I cried the terrible promise of the word love.

– III –

To whom the six speared star?
You have chosen and you but to whom shall be given
Jerusalem folded over and over in the green valley?
And to whom the sower
The greencoated fleshed ploughman
In the valley? You and you. To whom the green sword?
To whom the tree
Christed folded over and over, to
Whom Jerusalem? You and you.
The ploughman shall take the song into the valley
The greencoated farmer shall bring the sword into the valley
The eagle shall make a cry in the faithful country.
You and you and you.

–IV –

What may I give? Hours have been
Folded into this decision: others' wisdom given
That the gift may be given. What may I bring then?
That the giver and the loved shall be equal.
The farmer brings his seed to the valley
And neither is more equal more perfect.
What can I bring can I bring to the valley?
Only a green sword only the wish with it
Only my green coat that I clothe my thick flesh with.
And my song.
Why shall I bring *into* the valley?
Only my small seed only my forefathers' prayers
Only what lives in me as I lived then in them
Only the green whole song. I shall bring
That into the valley.
I shall be glad most glad to give that,
My life, my love, my Love!

– v –

Supposing time came out first from the belly of God
Our celebration of each new year
Or event, or endurance of the holy event
Would be a celebration of him.
And a love, like a new year
Would be of him also, a celebration,
A wind travelling from feast to feast
With the smell of wine and bread on it.
We must be always celebrating love as we celebrate God.
We must always love the new year
Turning in the lighted dark turning like the hands of music.
We must be like ploughmen and farmers in a valley
We must give our love a green coat and bring a song to her.
We must come out singing.
We must come out like a cry into the green world
We must come out singing with the charity of three beggars
We must come out with the marvellous open hands of music
We have to come out like three beggars, singing in the new year
For charity's sake
We must come out singing.

PROLOGUE

All the animals in my poems go into the ark
The human beings walk in the great dark
The bad dark and the good dark. They walk
Shivering under the small lamp light
And the road has two ways to go and the humans none.

The animals in my poems go into the ark.
The fox walks up with his vixen from the high hills
The wounded fly comes, the small dog, the black birds
And the red birds riding on the shining back of the sea:
They all come in from the flood like a holy circus.

The animals in my poems go into the ark.
There are two scrolls on the doors as they go
Which they cannot read. They are blessed for they walk in the dark
The good dark and the last dark, and they know
That human beings will hate them wherever they go.

EPILOGUE

All the people in my poems walk into the dark
All the animals walk up to the ark.
The people are deaf and limping like flies
Cunning shining soft sad they walk,
And they do not know but they walk into the bad dark.

All the animals in my poems walk in the sun
Blinking their eyes and licking their paws they go,
On and on up the proud procession of stairs
Up the proud straight stairs like a holy circus
And they do not know but they walk in the great light.

If all the people and all the animals
Joined dark with light, if all the proud people
And soft-stepping circus climbed their way in the dark
Walked with the black seals and walked with the spidery flies
They would all go into the great light, and they would know.

Part Two

ESTRANGEMENT AND CONTENTION

Thomas Hardy

« 1840 – 1928 »

BY THE EARTH'S CORPSE

– I –

"O Lord, why grievest Thou?—
  Since Life has ceased to be
Upon this globe, now cold
  As lunar land and sea,
And humankind, and fowl, and fur
  Are gone eternally,
All is the same to Thee as ere
  They knew mortality."

– II –

"O Time," replied the Lord,
  "Thou readest me ill, I ween;
Were all *the same,* I should not grieve
  At that late earthly scene,
Now blestly past—though planned by me
  With interest close and keen!—
Nay, nay: things now are *not* the same
  As they have earlier been.

– III –

  "Written indelibly
  On my eternal mind
  Are all the wrongs endured
  By earth's poor patient kind,
Which my too oft unconscious hand
  Let enter undesigned.
No god can cancel deeds foredone,
  Or thy old coils unwind!

– IV –

As when, in Noë's days,
I whelmed the plains with sea,
So at this last, when flesh
And herb but fossils be,
And, all extinct, their piteous dust
Revolves obliviously,
That I made Earth, and life, and man,
It still repenteth me!"

THE DARKLING THRUSH

I leant upon a coppice gate
When Frost was spectre-gray,
And Winter's dregs made desolate
The weakening eye of day.
The tangled bine-stems scored the sky
Like strings of broken lyres,
And all mankind that haunted nigh
Had sought their household fires.

The land's sharp features seemed to be
The Century's corpse outleant,
His crypt the cloudy canopy,
The wind his death-lament.
The ancient pulse of germ and birth
Was shrunken hard and dry,
And every spirit upon earth
Seemed fervourless as I.

At once a voice arose among
The bleak twigs overhead
In a full-hearted evensong
Of joy illimited;
An aged thrush, frail, gaunt, and small,
In blast-beruffled plume,
Had chosen thus to fling his soul
Upon the growing gloom.

So little cause for carolings
Of such ecstatic sound
Was written on terrestrial things
Afar or nigh around,
That I could think there trembled through
His happy good-night air
Some blessed Hope, whereof he knew
And I was unaware.

THE OXEN

Christmas Eve, and twelve of the clock.
'Now they are all on their knees,'
An elder said as we sat in a flock
By the embers in hearthside ease.

We pictured the meek mild creatures where
They dwelt in their strawy pen,
Nor did it occur to one of us there
To doubt they were kneeling then.

So fair a fancy few would weave
In these years! Yet, I feel,
If someone said on Christmas Eve,
'Come; see the oxen kneel,

'In the lonely barton by yonder coomb
Our childhood used to know,'
I should go with him in the gloom,
Hoping it might be so.

Gerard Manley Hopkins

« 1844 – 1889 »

SPELT FROM SIBYL'S LEAVES

Earnest, earthless, equal attuneable,ˈ vaulty, voluminous, . . . stupendous
Evening strains to be times vást,ˈ womb-of-all, home-of-all, hearse-of-all night.
Her fond yellow hornlight wound to the west,ˈ her wild hollow hoarlight hung to the height
Waste; her earliest stars, earl-stars,ˈ stárs principal, overbend us,
Fire-féaturing heaven. For earthˈ her being has unbound, her dapple is at an end, as-
tray or aswarm, all throughther, in throngs; self in self steepèd and páshed–qúite
Disremembering, dismémberingˈ all now. Heart, you round me right
With: Óur évening is over us; óur nightˈ whélms, whélms, ánd will end us.
Only the beak-leaves boughs dragonishˈ damask the tool-smooth bleak light; black,
Ever so black on it. Óur tale, O óur oracle!ˈ Lét life, wáned, ah lét life wind
Off hér once skéined stained véined varietyˈ upon, áll on twó spools; párt, pen, pack
Now her all in twó flocks, twó folds—black, white;ˈ right, wrong; reckon but, reck but, mind
But thése two; wáre of a wórld where bút theseˈ twó tell, each off the other; of a rack
Where, selfwrung, selfstrung, sheathe—and shelterless,ˈ thóughts agáinst thoughts in groans grind.

CARRION COMFORT

Not, I'll not, carrion comfort, Despair, not feast on thee;
Not untwist—slack they may be—these last strands of man
In me ór, most weary, cry *I can no more*. I can;
Can something, hope, wish day come, not choose not to be.
But ah, but O thou terrible, why wouldst thou rude on me
Thy wring-world right foot rock? lay a lionlimb against me? scan
With darksome devouring eyes my bruisèd bones? and fan,
O in turns of tempest, me heaped there; me frantic to avoid thee and flee?
Why? That my chaff might fly; my grain lie, sheer and clear.
Nay in all that toil, that coil, since (seems) I kissed the rod,
Hand rather, my heart lo! lapped strength, stole joy, would laugh, chéer.
Cheer whom though? the hero whose heaven-handling flung me, fóot tród
Me? or me that fought him? O which one? is it each one? That night,
that year
Of now done darkness I wretch lay wrestling with (my God!) my God.

William Butler Yeats

« 1865 – 1939 »

THE MAGI

Now as at all times I can see in the mind's eye,
In their stiff, painted clothes, the pale unsatisfied ones
Appear and disappear in the blue depth of the sky
With all their ancient faces like rain-beaten stones,
And all their helms of silver hovering side by side,
And all their eyes still fixed, hoping to find once more,
Being by Calvary's turbulence unsatisfied,
The uncontrollable mystery on the bestial floor.

Robert Frost

« 1874 - 1963 »

THE STRONG ARE SAYING NOTHING

The soil now gets a rumpling soft and damp,
And small regard to the future of any weed.
The final flat of the hoe's approval stamp
Is reserved for the bed of a few selected seed.

There is seldom more than a man to a harrowed piece.
Men work alone, their lots plowed far apart,
One stringing a chain of seed in an open crease,
And another stumbling after a halting cart.

To the fresh and black of the squares of early mold
The leafless bloom of a plum is fresh and white;
Though there's more than a doubt if the weather is not too cold
For the bees to come and serve its beauty aright.

Wind goes from farm to farm in wave on wave,
But carries no cry of what is hoped to be.
There may be little or much beyond the grave,
But the strong are saying nothing until they see.

FIRE AND ICE

Some say the world will end in fire,
Some say in ice.
From what I've tasted of desire
I hold with those who favor fire.

But if it had to perish twice,
I think I know enough of hate
To say that for destruction ice
Is also great
And would suffice.

BEREFT

Where had I heard this wind before
Change like this to a deeper roar?
What would it take my standing there for,
Holding open a restive door,
Looking down hill to a frothy shore?
Summer was past and day was past.
Somber clouds in the west were massed.
Out in the porch's sagging floor,
Leaves got up in a coil and hissed,
Blindly struck at my knee and missed.
Something sinister in the tone
Told me my secret must be known:
Word I was in the house alone
Somehow must have gotten abroad,
Word I was in my life alone,
Word I had no one left but God.

John Hall Wheelock

« 1886 – »

WOOD-THRUSH

Behind the wild bird's throat
An Eden, more remote
Than Adam knew of, lies—
The primal paradise
Lost, yet forever here,
From that wild syrinx cries
Into the listening ear,
The labyrinthine heart,
A longing, a regret,
In which it has no part.
Where the young leaves are met
In overarching green
Soft winds stir and divide,
Where shadows cloud and throng
The coverts in between,
That early bud of song
Opens its petals wide,
Becomes a three-fold star
Of voices twined and blent,
Happy and innocent,
Within whose singing are
Troy lost and Hector slain,
Judas and Golgotha,
The longing and the pain,
Sorrows of old that were
And joy come back again
From ages earlier,
Before joy's course was run,
Before time's bounds were set—

The fountains of the sun
Are in that twining jet
Of song, so clear, so cool.
While the false heart raves on,
For longing, like a fool,
The quiet voice is gone:
The song, inept to save,
Happy and innocent,
Falls silent as the grave,
Closing the door upon
Those half-remembered things—
Only the silence sings
On, and forever on.

Edwin Muir

« 1887 – 1959 »

THE ANIMALS

They do not live in the world,
Are not in time and space,
From birth to death hurled
No word do they have, not one
To plant a foot upon,
Were never in any place.

For with names the world was called
Out of the empty air,
With names was built and walled,
Line and circle and square,
Dust and emerald;
Snatched from deceiving death
By the articulate breath.

But these have never trod
Twice the familiar track,
Never never turned back
Into the memoried day.
All is new and near
In the unchanging Here
Of the fifth great day of God,
That shall remain the same,
Never shall pass away.

On the sixth day we came.

LOST AND FOUND

That by which we have lost and still shall lose
Even what we win (but never fully win,)
It gave the choice without the skill to choose,
The rough-cast world, the broken Eden within,
Taught us the narrow miss and the accident,
The countless odds and the predestined plot,
Action and thought to every bias bent,
And chance, the winning and the losing lot.

It gave us time, and time gave us the story,
Beginning and end in one wild largesse spent,
Inexplicable. Until the heavenly Glory
Took on our flesh and wrought the meaning. Since,
Sons, daughters, brothers, sisters of that Prince
Are we, by grace, although in banishment.

T. S. Eliot

« 1888 – »

THE HIPPOPOTAMUS

Similiter et omnes revereantur Diaconos, ut mandatum Jesu Christi; et Episcopum, ut Jesum Christum, existentem filium Patris; Presbyteros autem, ut concilium Dei et conjunctionem Apostolorum. Sine his Ecclesia non vocatur; de quibus suadeo vos sic habeo.

S. Ignatii Ad Trallianos.

And when this epistle is read among you, cause that it be read also in the church of the Laodiceans.

The broad-backed hippopotamus
Rests on his belly in the mud;
Although he seems so firm to us
He is merely flesh and blood.

Flesh and blood is weak and frail,
Susceptible to nervous shock;
While the True Church can never fail
For it is based upon a rock.

The hippo's feeble steps may err
In compassing material ends,
While the True Church need never stir
To gather in its dividends.

The 'potamus can never reach
The mango on the mango-tree;
But fruits of pomegranate and peach
Refresh the Church from over sea.

At mating time the hippo's voice
Betrays inflexions hoarse and odd,
But every week we hear rejoice
The Church, at being one with God.

The hippopotamus's day
Is passed in sleep; at night he hunts;
God works in a mysterious way—
The Church can sleep and feed at once.

I saw the 'potamus take wing
Ascending from the damp savannas,
And quiring angels round him sing
The praise of God, in loud hosannas.

Blood of the Lamb shall wash him clean
And him shall heavenly arms enfold,
Among the saints he shall be seen
Performing on a harp of gold.

He shall be washed as white as snow,
By all the martyr'd virgins kist,
While the True Church remains below
Wrapt in the old miasmal mist.

Conrad Aiken

« 1889 – »

TETÉLESTAI

– I –

How shall we praise the magnificence of the dead,
The great man humbled, the haughty brought to dust?
Is there a horn we should not blow as proudly
For the meanest of us all, who creeps his days,
Guarding his heart from blows, to die obscurely?
I am no king, have laid no kingdoms waste,
Taken no princess captive, led no triumphs
Of weeping women through long walls of trumpets;
Say rather, I am no one, or an atom;
Say rather, two great gods, in a vault of starlight,
Play ponderingly at chess, and at the game's end
One of the pieces, shaken, falls to the floor
And runs to the darkest corner; and that piece
Forgotten there, left motionless, is I . . .
Say that I have no name, no gifts, no power,
Am only one of millions, mostly silent;
One who came with eyes and hands and a heart,
Looked on beauty, and loved it, and then left it.
Say that the fates of time and space obscured me,
Led me a thousand ways to pain, bemused me,
Wrapped me in ugliness; and like great spiders
Dispatched me at their leisure . . . Well, what then?
Should I not hear, as I lie down in dust,
The horns of glory blowing above my burial?

– II –

Morning and evening opened and closed above me:
Houses were built above me; trees let fall

Yellowing leaves upon me, hands of ghosts;
Rain has showered its arrows of silver upon me
Seeking my heart; winds have roared and tossed me;
Music in long blue waves of sound has borne me
A helpless weed to shores of unthought silence;
Time, above me, within me, crashed its gongs
Of terrible warning, sifting the dust of death;
And here I lie. Blow now your horns of glory
Harshly over my flesh, you trees, you waters!
You stars and suns, Canopus, Deneb, Rigel,
Let me, as I die down, here in this dust,
Hear, far off, your whispered salutation!
Roar now above my decaying flesh, you winds,
Whirl out your earth-scents over this body, tell me
Of ferns and stagnant pools, wild roses, hillsides!
Anoint me, rain, let crash your silver arrows
On this hard flesh! I am the one who named you,
I lived in you, and now I die in you.
I your son, your daughter, treader of music,
Lie broken, conquered . . . Let me not fall in silence.

– III –

I, the restless one; the circler of circles;
Herdsman and roper of stars, who could not capture
The secret of self; I who was tyrant to weaklings,
Striker of children; destroyer of women; corrupter
Of innocent dreamers, and laugher at beauty; I,
Too easily brought to tears and weakness by music,
Baffled and broken by love, the helpless beholder
Of the war in my heart of desire with desire, the struggle
Of hatred with love, terror with hunger; I
Who laughed without knowing the cause of my laughter, who grew
Without wishing to grow, a servant to my own body;
Loved without reason the laughter and flesh of a woman,
Enduring such torments to find her! I who at last
Grow weaker, struggle more feebly, relent in my purpose,
Choose for my triumph an easier end, look backward
At earlier conquests; or, caught in the web, cry out
In a sudden and empty despair, 'Tetélestai!'
Pity me, now! I, who was arrogant, beg you!
Tell me, as I lie down, that I was courageous.

Blow horns of victory now, as I reel and am vanquished.
Shatter the sky with trumpets above my grave.

– IV –

. . . Look! this flesh how it crumbles to dust and is blown!
These bones, how they grind in the granite of frost and are nothing!
This skull, how it yawns for a flicker of time in the darkness,
Yet laughs not and sees not! It is crushed by a hammer of sunlight,
And the hands are destroyed . . . Press down through the leaves of the
    jasmine,
Dig through the interlaced roots—nevermore will you find me;
I was no better than dust, yet you cannot replace me. . . .
Take the soft dust in your hand—does it stir: does it sing?
Has it lips and a heart? Does it open its eyes to the sun?
Does it run, does it dream, does it burn with a secret, or tremble
In terror of death? or ache with tremendous decisions? . . .
Listen! . . . It says: 'I lean by the river. The willows
Are yellowed with bud. White clouds roar up from the south
And darken the ripples; but they cannot darken my heart,
Nor the face like a star in my heart! . . . Rain falls on the water
And pelts it, and rings it with silver. The willow trees glisten,
The sparrows chirp under the eaves; but the face in my heart
Is a secret of music . . . I wait in the rain and am silent.'
Listen again! . . . It says: 'I have worked, I am tired,
The pencil dulls in my hand: I see through the window
Walls upon walls of windows with faces behind them,
Smoke floating up to the sky, an ascension of sea-gulls.
I am tired. I have struggled in vain, my decision was fruitless,
Why then do I wait? with darkness, so easy, at hand! . . .
But tomorrow, perhaps . . . I will wait and endure till tomorrow!' . . .
Or again: 'It is dark. The decision is made. I am vanquished
By terror of life. The walls mount slowly about me
In coldness. I had not the courage. I was forsaken.
I cried out, was answered by silence . . . Tetélestai! . . .'

– V –

Hear how it babbles!—Blow the dust out of your hand,
With its voices and visions, tread on it, forget it, turn homeward
With dreams in your brain. . . . This, then, is the humble, the nameless,—
The lover, the husband and father, the struggler with shadows,
The one who went down under shoutings of chaos, the weakling

Who cried his 'forsaken!' like Christ on the darkening hilltop! . . .
This, then, is the one who implores, as he dwindles to silence,
A fanfare of glory. . . . And which of us dares to deny him?

PRELUDES FOR MEMNON

V

Despair, that seeking for the *Ding-an-sich,*
The feeling itself, the round bright dark emotion,
The color, the light, the depth, the feathery swiftness
Of you and the thought of you, I fall and fall
From precipice word to chasm word, and shatter
Heart, brain, and spirit on the maddening fact:
If poetry says it, it must speak with a symbol.

What is a symbol? It is the 'man stoops sharp
To clutch a paper that blows in the wind';
It is the 'bed of crocuses bending in the wind,' the
Light, that 'breaks on the water with waves,' the
Wings that 'achieve in the gust the unexpected.'
These, and less than these, and more than these.
The thought, the ghost of thought, the ghost in a mirror.

Catch a beam in your hands, a beam of light,
One bright golden beam, fledgling of dust,
Hold it a moment, and feel its heart, and feel
Ethereal pulse of light between your fingers:
Then let it escape from you, and find its home
In darkness, mother of light: and this will be
Symbol of symbol, clue to clue, auricle of heart.

The glass breaks, and the liquid is spilled; the string
Snaps, and the music stops; the moving cloud
Covers the sun, and the green field is dark.
These too are symbols: and as far and near
As those; they leave the silver core uneaten;
The golden leaf unplucked the bitter calyx
Virginal; and the whirling You unknown.

Allen Tate

« 1899 – »

THE CROSS

There is a place that some men know,
I cannot see the whole of it
Nor how I came there. Long ago
Flame burst out of a secret pit
Crushing the world with such a light
The day-sky fell to moonless black,
The kingly sun to hateful night
For those, once seeing, turning back:
For Love so hates mortality
Which is the providence of life
She will not let it blessèd be
But curses it with mortal strife,
Until beside the blinding rood
Within that world-destroying pit
—Like young wolves that have tasted blood,
Of death, men taste no more of it.
So blind, in so severe a place
(All life before in the black grave)
The last alternatives they face
Of life, without the life to save,
Being from all salvation weaned—
A stag charged both at heel and head:
Who would come back is turned a fiend
Instructed by the fiery dead.

Leonie Adams

« 1899 – »

THOSE NOT ELECT

Never, being damned, see paradise.
The heart will sweeten at its look;
Nor hell was known, till paradise
Our senses shook.

Never hear angels at laughter,
For how comports with grief to know
Wisdom in heaven bends to laughter, laughter,
Laughter upon woe?

Never fall dreaming on celestials,
Lest, bound in a ruinous place,
You turn to wander with celestials
Down holy space.

Never taste that fruit with the soul
Whereof the body may not eat,
Lest flesh at length lay waste the soul
In its sick heat.

Richard Eberhart

« 1904 – »

ORDER AND DISORDER

A passion came to me in the form of order,
To order all things in the mind.
Seek then frenzy, the foliating blood, then,
Seek the schisms of the stars, the will.

And did the passion come from order's self?
I heard in the wind the falling of a leaf.
And as the night's weak eye bore down on mine,
Was I its killer, was I its thief?

Strange things go on in the subtle night,
In the darkness the ages murmur and tremble.
Plato conceives, and Aristotle measures,
Buddha thinks deep, and Christ is burning white.

Each is an order, but each is a blight.
I feel my blood abounding, massive in darkness.
Each was an order, but each its order closing
In total harmony, save only Christ.

And the passion was a wild air of night,
It was a violation of the mind in its order,
A tumult, a transgression, ingression,
Christ's blood the strain in truth's disorder.

W. H. Auden

« 1907 – »

THE SHIELD OF ACHILLES

She looked over his shoulder
  For vines and olive trees,
Marble, well-governed cities,
  And ships upon untamed seas,
But there on the shining metal
  His hands had put instead
An artificial wilderness
  And a sky like lead.

A plain without a feature, bare and brown,
  No blade of grass, no sign of neighborhood,
Nothing to eat and nowhere to sit down,
  Yet, congregated on its blankness, stood
  An unintelligible multitude.
A million eyes, a million boots in line,
Without expression, waiting for a sign.

Out of the air a voice without a face
  Proved by statistics that some cause was just
In tones as dry and level as the place:
  No one was cheered and nothing was discussed;
  Column by column in a cloud of dust,
They marched away enduring a belief
Whose logic brought them, somewhere else, to grief.

She looked over his shoulder
  For ritual pieties,
White flower-garlanded heifers,
  Libation and sacrifice,

But there on the shining metal
  Where the altar should have been,
She saw by his flickering forge-light
  Quite another scene.

Barbed wire enclosed an arbitrary spot
  Where bored officials lounged (one cracked a joke)
And sentries sweated, for the day was hot:
  A crowd of ordinary decent folk
  Watched from without and neither moved nor spoke
As three pale figures were led forth and bound
To three posts driven upright in the ground.

The mass and majesty of this world, all
  That carries weight and always weighs the same,
Lay in the hands of others; they were small
  And could not hope for help and no help came:
  What their foes liked to do was done, their shame
Was all the worst could wish; they lost their pride
And died as men before their bodies died.

She looked over his shoulder
  For athletes at their games,
Men and women in a dance
  Moving their sweet limbs
Quick, quick, to music,
  But there on the shining shield
His hands had set no dancing-floor
  But a weed-choked field.

A ragged urchin, aimless and alone,
  Loitered about that vacancy; a bird
Flew up to safety from his well-aimed stone:
  That girls are raped, that two boys knife a third,
  Were axioms to him, who'd never heard
Of any world where promises were kept
Or one could weep because another wept.

The thin-lipped armorer,
  Hephaestos, hobbled away;
Thetis of the shining breasts
  Cried out in dismay

At what the God had wrought
  To please her son, the strong
Iron-hearted man-slaying Achilles
  Who would not live long.

PRIME (from "Horae Canonicae")

Simultaneously, as soundlessly,
  Spontaneously, suddenly
As, at the vaunt of the dawn, the kind
  Gates of the body fly open
To its world beyond, the gates of the mind,
  The horn gate and the ivory gate,
Swing to, swing shut, instantaneously
  Quell the nocturnal rummage
Of its rebellious fronde, ill-favored,
  Ill-natured and second-rate,
Disenfranchised, widowed and orphaned
  By an historical mistake:
Recalled from the shades to be a seeing being,
  From absence to be on display,
Without a name or history I wake
  Between my body and the day.

Holy this moment, wholly in the right,
  As, in complete obedience
To the light's laconic outcry, next
  As a sheet, near as a wall,
Out there as a mountain's poise of stone,
  The world is present, about,
And I know that I am, here, not alone
  But with a world, and rejoice
Unvexed, for the will has still to claim
  This adjacent arm as my own,
The memory to name me, resume
  Its routine of praise and blame,
And smiling to me is this instant while
  Still the day is intact, and I

The Adam sinless in our beginning,
  Adam still previous to any act.

I draw breath; that is of course to wish
  No matter what, to be wise,
To be different, to die and the cost,
  No matter how, is Paradise
Lost of course and myself owing a death:
  The eager ridge, the steady sea,
The flat roofs of the fishing village
  Still asleep in its bunny,
Though as fresh and sunny still, are not friends
  But things to hand, this ready flesh
No honest equal but my accomplice now,
  My assassin to be, and my name
Stands for my historical share of care
  For a lying self-made city,
Afraid of our living task, the dying
  Which the coming day will ask.

Dylan Thomas

« 1914 – 1953 »

A REFUSAL TO MOURN THE DEATH, BY FIRE, OF A CHILD IN LONDON

Never until the mankind making
Bird beast and flower
Fathering and all humbling darkness
Tells with silence the last light breaking
And the still hour
Is come of the sea tumbling in harness

And I must enter again the round
Zion of the water bead
And the synagogue of the ear of corn
Shall I let pray the shadow of a sound
Or sow my salt seed
In the least valley of sackcloth to mourn

The majesty and burning of the child's death.
I shall not murder
The mankind of her going with a grave truth
Nor blaspheme down the stations of the breath
With any further
Elegy of innocence and youth.

Deep with the first dead lies London's daughter,
Robed in the long friends,
The grains beyond age, the dark veins of her mother
Secret by the unmourning water
Of the riding Thames.
After the first death, there is no other.

Cecil Hemley

« 1914 – »

MY ABSENT GOD

My absent God does not disown
That timeless joy He lives alone;
He does not seek as once His own.

But should He change and dive from night
As swan or eagle, would the might
Of creature wings give me insight?

Would loving talons rip despair,
And make the ways of violence clear?
Would holy eyes their vision share?

Or if again, a bush in flame,
He burned into my brain His name,
Would I accept this stranger's claim?

IF HE WERE ANYWHERE

I would be His if He were anywhere;
If He were anything He would appear.

If He had any name the name I give
Would find Him in the night and make Him live.

But He is nameless, nothing, and nowhere,
Beyond concern with me and my despair.

And, naming Him, I only name my wish:
To break from bone and live in spirit's flesh.

And, seeking Him, still trammeled in the mind,
I dare not leave my selfish name behind.

That which is actual does not endure;
He will not have me till I forfeit more.

Robert Lowell

« 1917 – »

THE HOLY INNOCENTS

Listen, the hay-bells tinkle as the cart
Wavers on rubber tires along the tar
And cindered ice below the burlap mill
And ale-wife run. The oxen drool and start
In wonder at the fenders of a car,
And blunder hugely up St. Peter's hill.
These are the undefiled by woman—their
Sorrow is not the sorrow of this world:
King Herod shrieking vengeance at the curled
Up knees of Jesus choking in the air,

A king of speechless clods and infants. Still
The world out-Herods Herod; and the year,
The nineteen-hundred forty-fifth of grace,
Lumbers with losses up the clinkered hill
Of our purgation; and the oxen near
The worn foundations of their resting-place,
The holy manger where their bed is corn
And holly torn for Christmas. If they die,
As Jesus, in the harness, who will mourn?
Lamb of the shepherds, Child, how still you lie.

CHRISTMAS EVE UNDER HOOKER'S STATUE

Tonight a blackout. Twenty years ago
I hung my stocking on the tree, and hell's
Serpent entwined the apple in the toe

To sting the child with knowledge. Hooker's heels
Kicking at nothing in the shifting snow,
A cannon and a cairn of cannon balls
Rusting before the blackened Statehouse, know
How the long horn of plenty broke like glass
In Hooker's gauntlets. Once I came from Mass;

Now storm-clouds shelter Christmas, once again
Mars meets his fruitless star with open arms,
His heavy saber flashes with the rime,
The war-god's bronzed and empty forehead forms
Anonymous machinery from raw men;
The cannon on the Common cannot stun
The blundering butcher as he rides on Time—
The barrel clinks with holly. I am cold:
I ask for bread, my father gives me mould;

His stocking is full of stones. Santa in red
Is crowned with wizened berries. Man of war,
Where is the summer's garden? In its bed
The ancient speckled serpent will appear,
And black-eyed susan with her frizzled head.
When Chancellorsville mowed down the volunteer,
"All wars are boyish," Herman Melville said;
But we are old, our fields are running wild:
Till Christ again turn wanderer and child.

AS A PLANE TREE BY THE WATER

Darkness has called to darkness, and disgrace
Elbows about our windows in this planned
Babel of Boston where our money talks
And multiplies the darkness of a land
Of preparation where the Virgin walks
And roses spiral her enamelled face
Or fall to splinters on unwatered streets.
Our Lady of Babylon, go by, go by,
I was once the apple of your eye;
Flies, flies are on the plane tree, on the streets.

The flies, the flies, the flies of Babylon
Buzz in my ear-drums while the devil's long
Dirge of the people detonates the hour
For floating cities where his golden tongue
Enchants the masons of the Babel Tower
To raise tomorrow's city to the sun
That never sets upon these hell-fire streets
Of Boston, where the sunlight is a sword
Striking at the withholder of the Lord:
Flies, flies are on the plane tree, on the streets.

Flies strike the miraculous waters of the iced
Atlantic and the eyes of Bernadette
Who saw Our Lady standing in the cave
At Massabielle, saw her so squarely that
Her vision put out reason's eyes. The grave
Is open-mouthed and swallowed up in Christ.
O walls of Jericho! And all the streets
To our Atlantic wall are singing: "Sing,
Sing for the resurrection of the King."
Flies, flies are on the plane tree, on the streets.

Anne Sexton

« 1928 – »

FOR GOD WHILE SLEEPING

Sleeping in fever, I am unfit
to know just who you are:
hung up like a pig on exhibit,
the delicate wrists,
the beard drooling blood and vinegar;
hooked to your own weight,
jolting toward death under your nameplate.

Everyone in this crowd needs a bath.
I am dressed in rags.
The mother wears blue. You grind your teeth
and with each new breath
your jaws gape and your diaper sags.
I am not to blame
for all this. I do not know your name.

Skinny man, you are somebody's fault.
You ride on dark poles—
a wooden bird that a trader built
for some fool who felt
that he could make the flight. Now you roll
in your sleep, seasick
on your own breathing, poor old convict.

Ted Hughes

« 1930 – »

COMPLAINT

Aged Mother, Mary, even though—when that thing
Leaped hedge in the dark lane (or grabbed your heel
On the attic stair) by smell of man and coarse
Canvas he wore was disguised too well-ill
A scorching and dizzying blue apparition;—

Though that Jack Horner's hedge-scratched pig-splitting arm,
Grubbing his get among your lilies, was a comet
That plunged through the flowery whorl to your womb-root,
And grew a man's face on its burning head;—

Though no prompt thundercrack, no knave's remorse
Kneeling in the arch of lightning, fisting his guilt,
But the times quiet with God's satisfaction;—

Though you swallowed the honey of a parable,
No forced fistful of meat-and-potato fact—

History's grown gross-bellied, not bright-eyed.

Jon Silkin

« 1930 – »

FIRST IT WAS SINGING

From the first cry
I was given music with which to speak,
Tramping the staring streets
The amazed faces

Turning, laughing with their
Windy voices at the mad singer in the common
Street. From the first I was
Given a voice

To cry out with.
It was music, bread, blood, singing, love.
Afterwards it was dying
But it was singing

First.
And from that it was I loved the hopping birds,
The limping fly
And the mad

Bee, stung to anger
In worship of summer. It was their speech and my speech,
The Jewish stone and the
Animal rock

Rolling together that made me sing
Of our common lash, the great white weal across
Our black back, I and the hunted
Fox, I and the huge

Fly, his dangerous wings
Torn from his villainous body, I and the seal
Harming the human sea with his song,
I and the bawling dog.

It was our harm
Made me sing. Afterwards it was death,
Afterwards it was our death,
Death of the stone

By stoning, the animal
By animals, but, first, singing,
Jew and animal singing first.
And afterwards death.

THE TWO FREEDOMS

There were two birds today
Broke from their cage and seemed as gold until
In the dry sun, their bodies were
Transfigured; they hung like ghosts possessed with the silence
But not with the shapelessness of
Spirits; they, in the sun flashed one gold flown

Through another;
And then were quiet on the broad, trunked back
Of the wood chair. They were
Inviolable, with that power and helplessness
Which sculpture has. The sunlight
Smoked on them, gold were their wings, gold feet; gold sounds

Fled from their throats quickened by
The winged sun that, for a moment, urged their flesh
To the transubstantial freedom
Ghosts are. They in the sun became the one gold
With him in dignity.
I caught and put them back into their cage.

Surely, I thought, Man is
Ridiculous whose avarice for life
Is that he must put life
Back in a cage, cage life; he will increase
The flow of the cruel gland,
Then watch, then feel his power and its rage

Grow and be satisfied.
I shut the cage door, I looked with a cold rage
At their stretched screams of pain,
And I thought again of the stairs down which the world
Turns from its prison to
The cage of the still prison; turns and is caged.

And thought, but it is best
That they fly in their cage and do not learn
Of that grey, ironic flight
From one space to another, but step down
From their carriage in the air
To that humble, iron house. Safely the breast

Has shed that gold
Which had perched, for an instant, on their flesh.
But as these careful words
Turned in my mind, their cry like a stab pierced
Me; I thought of my own
Wings, cut and trimmed by my grey God.

AND I TURNED FROM THE INNER HEART

And I turned from the inner heart having no further cause
To look there, to pursue what lay inside,
And moved to the world not as I would have world
But as it lay before me, as a map lies open
Unalterable through what it signifies, without vision
Or fantasy, yet full with promise. And although

The world as I had known it I replenished
Only with the dreams of the man who lies in sickness
Although I believed in that reconstruction of hope
I knew that world, as replete with misery
As the bowl the beggar raises, empty, yet full
With the dried bones of starvation, as the cup denied

Milk, death before milk; and I turned to the outer
Place, although as I knew I could not hope
To care for those who were there, neither for what they
might be
Nor for what they were, meanness scrubbed into the face
The naked bone of the face in sleep
Not tender now nor cruel but as the stone,

Instrument to be used, to be kept sharp for
The brass fiction of the Industrial King
Who is inviolate; but who is yet intact
From Human Agony. So that I cried, Lord,
I am not supreme with your Word, but regard now
Your tin world. Is *this* your vision? Straightway the whirr

Of the indefatigable machine filled the wheel-dark air.
And the worker cried, 'This is the terrible, real world
Of the beggar's bowl, which lies empty, world whose image is
Refracted by a brass screw. Our dreams are wound
Within the coil of tungsten. The beggar's bowls are broken;
But our world lies open like a map of hope!'

Sylvia Plath

« 1932 – 1963 »

BLACK ROOK IN RAINY WEATHER

On the stiff twig up there
Hunches a wet black rook
Arranging and rearranging its feathers in the rain.
I do not expect miracle
Or an accident

To set the sight on fire
In my eye, nor seek
Any more in the desultory weather some design,
But let spotted leaves fall as they fall,
Without ceremony, or portent.

Although, I admit, I desire,
Occasionally, some backtalk
From the mute sky, I can't honestly complain:
A certain minor light may still
Leap incandescent

Out of kitchen table or chair
As if a celestial burning took
Possession of the most obtuse objects now and then—
Thus hallowing an interval
Otherwise inconsequent

By bestowing largesse, honour,
One might say love. At any rate, I now walk
Wary (for it could happen
Even in this dull, ruinous landscape); sceptical,
Yet politic; ignorant

Of whatever angel may choose to flare
Suddenly at my elbow. I only know that a rook
Ordering its black feathers can so shine
As to seize my senses, haul
My eyelids up, and grant

A brief respite from fear
Of total neutrality. With luck,
Trekking stubborn through this season
Of fatigue, I shall
Patch together a content

Of sorts. Miracles occur,
If you care to call those spasmodic
Tricks of radiance miracles. The wait's begun again,
The long wait for the angel,
For that rare, random descent.

Part Three

MEDITATION AND SPIRITUAL JOURNEY

Gerard Manley Hopkins

« 1844 - 1889 »

THE LEADEN ECHO AND THE GOLDEN ECHO

(Maidens' Song from St. Winefred's Well)

– THE LEADEN ECHO –

How to kéep—is there ány any, is there none such, nowhere known some, bow or brooch or braid or brace, láce, latch or catch or key to keep
Back beauty, keep it, beauty, beauty, beauty, . . . from vanishing away?
Ó is there no frowning of these wrinkles, rankèd wrinkles deep,
Dówn? no waving off of these most mournful messengers, still messengers, sad and stealing messengers of grey?
No there's none, there's none, O no there's none,
Nor can you long be, what you now are, called fair,
Do what you may do, what, do what you may,
And wisdom is early to despair:
Be beginning; since, no, nothing can be done to keep at bay
Age and age's evils, hoar hair,
Ruck and wrinkle, drooping, dying, death's worst, winding sheets, tombs and worms and tumbling to decay;
So be beginning, be beginning to despair.
O there's none; no no no there's none:
Be beginning to despair, to despair,
Despair, despair, despair, despair.

– THE GOLDEN ECHO –

Spare!
There is one, yes I have one (Hush there!);
Only not within seeing of the sun,
Not within the singeing of the strong sun,
Tall sun's tingeing, or treacherous the tainting of the earth's air,
Somewhere elsewhere there is ah well where! one,

Ońe. Yes I cán tell such a key, I dó know such a place,
Where whatever's prized and passes of us, everything that's fresh and fast flying of us, seems to us sweet of us and swiftly away with, done away with, undone,
Úndone, done with, soon done with, and yet dearly and dangerously sweet
Of us, the wimpled-water-dimpled, not-by-morning-matchèd face,
The flower of beauty, fleece of beauty, too too apt to, ah! to fleet,
Never fleets móre, fastened with the tenderest truth
To its own best being and its loveliness of youth: it is an everlastingness of, O it is an all youth!
Come then, your ways and airs and looks, locks, maiden gear, gallantry and gaiety and grace,
Winning ways, airs innocent, maiden manners, sweet looks, loose locks, long locks, lovelocks, gaygear, going gallant, girlgrace—
Resign them, sign them, send them, motion them with breath,
And with sighs soaring, soaring síghs deliver
Them; beauty-in-thee-ghost, deliver it, early now, long before death
Give beauty back, beauty, beauty, beauty, back to God, beauty's self and beauty's giver.

See; not a hair is, not an eyelash, not the least lash lost; every hair
Is, hair of the head, numbered.
Nay, what we had lighthanded left in surly the mere mould
Will have waked and have waxed and have walked with the wind whatwhile we slept,
This side, that side hurling a heavyheaded hundredfold
Whatwhile we, while we slumbered.
O then, weary then whý should we tread? O why are we so haggard at the heart, so care-coiled, care-killed, so fagged, so fashed, so cogged, so cumbered,
When the thing we freely fórfeit is kept with fonder a care,

Fonder a care kept than we could have kept it, kept
Far with fonder a care (and we, we should have lost it) finer, fonder
A care kept.—Where kept? Do but tell us where kept, where.—
Yonder.—What high as that! We follow, now we follow.—Yonder, yes yonder, yonder,
Yonder.

William Butler Yeats

« 1865 - 1939 »

SAILING TO BYZANTIUM

I

That is no country for old men. The young
In one another's arms, birds in the trees
—Those dying generations—at their song,
The salmon-falls, the mackerel-crowded seas,
Fish, flesh, or fowl, commend all summer long
Whatever is begotten, born, and dies.
Caught in that sensual music all neglect
Monuments of unageing intellect.

II

An aged man is but a paltry thing,
A tattered coat upon a stick, unless
Soul clap its hands and sing, and louder sing
For every tatter in its mortal dress,
Nor is there singing school but studying
Monuments of its own magnificence;
And therefore I have sailed the seas and come
To the holy city of Byzantium.

III

O sages standing in God's holy fire
As in the gold mosaic of a wall,
Come from the holy fire, perne in a gyre,
And be the singing-masters of my soul.
Consume my heart away; sick with desire
And fastened to a dying animal
It knows not what it is; and gather me
Into the artifice of eternity.

IV

Once out of nature I shall never take
My bodily form from any natural thing,
But such a form as Grecian goldsmiths make
Of hammered gold and gold enamelling
To keep a drowsy Emperor awake;
Or set upon a golden bough to sing
To lords and ladies of Byzantium
Of what is past, or passing, or to come.

VACILLATION

– I –

Between extremities
Man runs his course;
A brand, or flaming breath,
Comes to destroy
All those antinomies
Of day and night;
The body calls it death,
The heart remorse.
But if these be right
What is joy?

– II –

A tree there is that from its topmost bough
Is half all glittering flame and half all green
Abounding foliage moistened with the dew;
And half is half and yet is all the scene;
And half and half consume what they renew,
And he that Attis' image hangs between
That staring fury and the blind lush leaf
May know not what he knows, but knows not grief.

– III –

Get all the gold and silver that you can,
Satisfy ambition, animate
The trivial days and ram them with the sun,
And yet upon these maxims meditate:
All women dote upon an idle man
Although their children need a rich estate;
No man has ever lived that had enough
Of children's gratitude or woman's love.
No longer in Lethean foliage caught
Begin the preparation for your death
And from the fortieth winter by that thought
Test every work of intellect or faith,
And everything that your own hands have wrought,
And call those works extravagance of breath
That are not suited for such men as come
Proud, open-eyed and laughing to the tomb.

– IV –

My fiftieth year had come and gone,
I sat, a solitary man,
In a crowded London shop,
An open book and empty cup
On the marble table-top.
While on the shop and street I gazed
My body of a sudden blazed;
And twenty minutes more or less
It seemed, so great my happiness,
That I was blessèd and could bless.

– V –

Although the summer sunlight gild
Cloudy leafage of the sky,
Or wintry moonlight sink the field
In storm-scattered intricacy,
I cannot look thereon,
Responsibility so weighs me down.
Things said or done long years ago,
Or things I did not do or say
But thought that I might say or do,

Weigh me down, and not a day
But something is recalled,
My conscience or my vanity appalled.

– VI –

A rivery field spread out below,
An odour of the new-mown hay
In his nostrils, the great lord of Chou
Cried, casting off the mountain snow
'Let all things pass away.'
Wheels by milk-white asses drawn
Where Babylon or Nineveh
Rose; some conqueror drew rein
And cried to battle-weary men,
'Let all things pass away.'
From man's blood-sodden heart are sprung
Those branches of the night and day
Where the gaudy moon is hung.
What's the meaning of all song?
'Let all things pass away.'

– VII –

The Soul. Seek out reality, leave things that seem.
The Heart. What, be a singer born and lack a theme?
The Soul. Isaiah's coal, what more can man desire?
The Heart. Struck dumb in the simplicity of fire!
The Soul. Look on that fire, salvation walks within.
The Heart. What theme had Homer but original sin?

– VIII –

Must we part, Von Hügel, though much alike, for we
Accept the miracles of the saints and honour sanctity?
The body of Saint Teresa lies undecayed in tomb,
Bathed in miraculous oil, sweet odours from it come,
Healing from its lettered slab. Those self-same hands perchance
Eternalised the body of a modern saint that once
Had scooped out Pharaoh's mummy. I—though heart might find relief

Did I become a Christian man and choose for my belief
What seems most welcome in the tomb—play a
  predestined part.
Homer is my example and his unchristened heart.
The lion and the honeycomb, what has Scripture said?
So get you gone, Von Hügel, though with blessings on
  your head.

Edwin Arlington Robinson

« 1869 – 1935 »

THE WANDERING JEW

I saw by looking in his eyes
That they remembered everything;
And this was how I came to know
That he was here, still wandering.
For though the figure and the scene
Were never to be reconciled,
I knew the man as I had known
His image when I was a child.

With evidence at every turn,
I should have held it safe to guess
That all the newness of New York
Had nothing new in loneliness;
Yet here was one who might be Noah,
Or Nathan, or Abimelech,
Or Lamech, out of ages lost,—
Or, more than all, Melchizedek.

Assured that he was none of these,
I gave them back their names again,
To scan once more those endless eyes
Where all my questions ended then.
I found in them what they revealed
That I shall not live to forget,
And wondered if they found in mine
Compassion that I might regret.

Pity, I learned, was not the least
Of time's offending benefits
That had now for so long impugned

The conservation of his wits:
Rather it was that I should yield,
Alone, the fealty that presents
The tribute of a tempered ear
To an untempered eloquence.

Before I pondered long enough
On whence he came and who he was,
I trembled at his ringing wealth
Of manifold anathemas;
I wondered, while he seared the world,
What new defection ailed the race,
And if it mattered how remote
Our fathers were from such a place.

Before there was an hour for me
To contemplate with less concern
The crumbling realm awaiting us
Than his that was beyond return,
A dawning on the dust of years
Had shaped with an elusive light
Mirages of remembered scenes
That were no longer for the sight.

For now the gloom that hid the man
Became a daylight on his wrath,
And one wherein my fancy viewed
New lions ramping in his path.
The old were dead and had no fangs,
Wherefore he loved them—seeing not
They were the same that in their time
Had eaten everything they caught.

The world around him was a gift
Of anguish to his eyes and ears,
And one that he had long reviled
As fit for devils, not for seers.
Where, then, was there a place for him
That on this other side of death
Saw nothing good, as he had seen
No good come out of Nazareth?

Yet here there was a reticence,
And I believe his only one,
That hushed him as if he beheld
A Presence that would not be gone.
In such a silence he confessed
How much there was to be denied;
And he would look at me and live,
As others might have looked and died.

As if at last he knew again
That he had always known, his eyes
Were like to those of one who gazed
On those of One who never dies.
For such a moment he revealed
What life has in it to be lost;
And I could ask if what I saw,
Before me there, was man or ghost.

He may have died so many times
That all there was of him to see
Was pride, that kept itself alive
As too rebellious to be free;
He may have told, when more than once
Humility seemed imminent,
How many a lonely time in vain
The Second Coming came and went.

Whether he still defies or not
The failure of an angry task
That relegates him out of time
To chaos, I can only ask.
But as I knew him, so he was;
And somewhere among men to-day
Those old, unyielding eyes may flash,
And flinch—and look the other way.

LUKE HAVERGAL

Go to the western gate, Luke Havergal,
There where the vines cling crimson on the wall,
And in the twilight wait for what will come.
The leaves will whisper there of her, and some,
Like flying words, will strike you as they fall;
But go, and if you listen she will call.
Go to the western gate, Luke Havergal—
Luke Havergal.

No, there is not a dawn in eastern skies
To rift the fiery night that's in your eyes;
But there, where western glooms are gathering,
The dark will end the dark, if anything:
God slays himself with every leaf that flies,
And hell is more than half of paradise.
No, there is not a dawn in eastern skies—
In eastern skies.

Out of a grave I come to tell you this,
Out of a grave I come to quench the kiss
That flames upon your forehead with a glow
That blinds you to the way that you must go.
Yes, there is yet one way to where she is,
Bitter, but one that faith may never miss.
Out of a grave I come to tell you this—
To tell you this.

There is the western gate, Luke Havergal,
There are the crimson leaves upon the wall.
Go, for the winds are tearing them away,—
Nor think to riddle the dead words they say,
Nor any more to feel them as they fall;
But go, and if you trust her she will call.
There is the western gate, Luke Havergal—
Luke Havergal.

Robert Frost

« 1874 – 1963 »

DIRECTIVE

Back out of all this now too much for us,
Back in a time made simple by the loss
Of detail, burned, dissolved, and broken off
Like graveyard marble sculpture in the weather,
There is a house that is no more a house
Upon a farm that is no more a farm
And in a town that is no more a town.
The road there, if you'll let a guide direct you
Who only has at heart your getting lost,
May seem as if it should have been a quarry—
Great monolithic knees the former town
Long since gave up pretence of keeping covered.
And there's a story in a book about it:
Besides the wear of iron wagon wheels
The ledges show lines ruled southeast northwest,
The chisel work of an enormous Glacier
That braced his feet against the Arctic Pole.
You must not mind a certain coolness from him
Still said to haunt this side of Panther Mountain.
Nor need you mind the serial ordeal
Of being watched from forty cellar holes
As if by eye pairs out of forty firkins.
As for the woods' excitement over you
That sends light rustle rushes to their leaves,
Charge that to upstart inexperience.
Where were they all not twenty years ago?
They think too much of having shaded out
A few old pecker-fretted apple trees.
Make yourself up a cheering song of how
Someone's road home from work this once was,

Who may be just ahead of you on foot
Or creaking with a buggy load of grain.
The height of the adventure is the height
Of country where two village cultures faded
Into each other. Both of them are lost.
And if you're lost enough to find yourself
By now, pull in your ladder road behind you
And put a sign up CLOSED to all but me.
Then make yourself at home. The only field
Now left's no bigger than a harness gall.
First there's the children's house of make believe,
Some shattered dishes underneath a pine,
The playthings in the playhouse of the children.
Weep for what little things could make them glad.
Then for the house that is no more a house,
But only a belilaced cellar hole,
Now slowly closing like a dent in dough.
This was no playhouse but a house in earnest.
Your destination and your destiny's
A brook that was the water of the house,
Cold as a spring as yet so near its source,
Too lofty and original to rage.
(We know the valley streams that when aroused
Will leave their tatters hung on barb and thorn.)
I have kept hidden in the instep arch
Of an old cedar at the waterside
A broken drinking goblet like the Grail
Under a spell so the wrong ones can't find it,
So can't get saved, as Saint Mark says they mustn't.
(I stole the goblet from the children's playhouse.)
Here are your waters and your watering place.
Drink and be whole again beyond confusion.

REVELATION

We make ourselves a place apart
  Behind light words that tease and flout,
But oh, the agitated heart
  Till someone really find us out.

'Tis pity if the case require
  (Or so we say) that in the end
We speak the literal to inspire
  The understanding of a friend.

But so with all, from babes that play
  At hide-and-seek to God afar,
So all who hide too well away
  Must speak and tell us where they are.

DESIGN

I found a dimpled spider, fat and white,
On a white heal-all, holding up a moth
Like a white piece of rigid satin cloth—
Assorted characters of death and blight
Mixed ready to begin the morning right,
Like the ingredients of a witches' broth—
A snow-drop spider, a flower like froth,
And dead wings carried like a paper kite.
What had that flower to do with being white,
The wayside blue and innocent heal-all?
What brought the kindred spider to that height,
Then steered the white moth thither in the night?
What but design of darkness to appall?—
If design govern in a thing so small.

THE SILKEN TENT

She is as in a field a silken tent
At midday when a sunny summer breeze
Has dried the dew and all its ropes relent,
So that in guys it gently sways at ease,
And its supporting central cedar pole,
That is its pinnacle to heavenward

And signifies the sureness of the soul,
Seems to owe naught to any single cord,
But strictly held by none, is loosely bound
But countless silken ties of love and thought
To everything on earth the compass round,
And only by one's going slightly taut
In the capriciousness of summer air
Is of the slightest bondage made aware.

ONCE BY THE PACIFIC

The shattered water made a misty din.
Great waves looked over others coming in,
And thought of doing something to the shore
That water never did to land before.
The clouds were low and hairy in the skies,
Like locks blown forward in the gleam of eyes.
You could not tell, and yet it looked as if
The shore was lucky in being backed by cliff,
The cliff in being backed by continent;
It looked as if a night of dark intent
Was coming, and not only a night, an age.
Someone had better be prepared for rage.
There would be more than ocean-water broken
Before God's last *Put out the Light* was spoken.

James Stephens

« 1882 – 1950 »

THE GOAT PATHS

– 1 –

The crooked paths
Go every way
Upon the hill
—They wind about
Through the heather,
In and out
Of a quiet
Sunniness.

And the goats,
Day after day,
Stray
In sunny
Quietness;
Cropping here,
And cropping there
—As they pause,
And turn,
And pass—
Now a bit
Of heather spray,
Now a mouthful
Of the grass.

– 2 –

In the deeper
Sunniness;

In the place
Where nothing stirs;
Quietly
In quietness;
In the quiet
Of the furze
They stand a while;
They dream;
They lie;
They stare
Upon the roving sky.

If you approach
They run away!
They will stare,
And stamp,
And bound,
With a sudden angry sound,
To the sunny
Quietude;
To crouch again,
Where nothing stirs,
In the quiet
Of the furze:
To crouch them down again,
And brood,
In the sunny
Solitude.

– 3 –

Were I but
As free
As they,
I would stray
Away
And brood;
I would beat
A hidden way,
Through the quiet
Heather spray,

To a sunny
Solitude.

And should you come
I'd run away!
I would make an angry sound,
I would stare,
And stamp,
And bound
To the deeper
Quietude;
To the place
Where nothing stirs
In the quiet
Of the furze.

– 4 –

In that airy
Quietness
I would dream
As long as they:
Through the quiet
Sunniness
I would stray
Away
And brood,
All among
The heather spray,
In a sunny
Solitude.

—I would think
Until I found
Something
I can never find;
—Something
Lying
On the ground,
In the bottom
Of my mind.

THE WATCHER

A rose for a young head,
A ring for a bride,
Joy for the homestead
Clean and wide
—Who's that waiting
In the rain outside?

A heart for an old friend,
A hand for the new:
Love can to earth lend
Heaven's hue—
—Who's that standing
In the silver dew?

A smile for the parting,
A tear as they go,
God's sweethearting
Ends just so—
—Who's that watching
Where the black winds blow?

He who is waiting
In the rain outside,
He who is standing
Where the dew drops wide,
He who is watching
In the wind must ride

—Tho' the pale hands cling—
With the rose, and the ring,
And the bride;
Must ride,
With the red of the rose,
And the gold of the ring,
And the lips and the hair of the bride.

William Carlos Williams

« 1883 – 1963 »

THE GARDEN

IT IS FAR TO ASSISI,

but not too far:
Over this garden,
brooding over this garden,
there is a kindly spirit,
brother to the poor
and who is poorer than he
who is in love
when birds are nesting
in the spring of the year?
They came
to eat from his hand
who had nothing,
and yet
from his plenty
he fed them all.
All mankind
grew to be his debtors,
a simple story.
Love is in season.

AT SUCH A TIME,
hyacinth time
in
the hospital garden,
the time
of the coral flowered

and early salmon pink
clusters, it is
the time also of
abandoned birds' nests
before
the sparrows start
to tear them apart
against the advent of that bounty
from which
they will build anew.

ALL ABOUT THEM

on the lawns
the young couples
embrace
as in a tale
by Boccaccio
They are careless
under license of the disease
which has restricted them
to these grounds.
St. Francis forgive them
and all lovers
whoever they may be.
They have seen
a great light, it
springs from their own bawdy foreheads.
The light
is sequestered there
by these enclosing walls.
They are divided
from their fellows.
It is a bounty
from last year's nest.
St. Francis,
who befriended the wild birds,
by their aid,
those who
have nothing,
and live
by the Holy light of love

that rules,
blocking despair,
over this garden.

TIME PASSES.
The pace has slackened
But with the falling off
of the pace
the scene has altered.
The lovers raise their heads,
at that which has come over them.
It is summer now.
The broad sun
shines!
Blinded by the light
they walk bewildered,
seeking
between the leaves
for a vantage
from which to view
the advancing season.
They are incredulous
of their own cure
and half minded
to escape
into the dark again.
The scene
indeed has changed.
By St. Francis
the whole scene
has changed.
They glimpse
a surrounding sky
and the whole countryside.
Filled with terror
they seek
a familiar flower
at which to warm themselves,
but the whole field
accosts them.

They hide their eyes
ashamed
before that bounty,
peering through their fingers
timidly.
The saint is watching,
his eyes filled with pity.

THE YEAR IS STILL young
but not so young
as they
who face the fears
with which
they are confronted.
Reawakened
after love's first folly
they resemble children
roused from a long sleep.
Summer is here,
right enough.
The saint
has tactfully withdrawn.
One
emboldened,
parting the leaves before her,
stands in the full sunlight,
alone
shading her eyes
as her heart
beats wildly
and her mind
drinks up
the full meaning
of it
all!

Robinson Jeffers

« 1887 – 1962 »

THE WORLD'S WONDERS

Being now three or four years more than sixty,
I have seen strange things in my time. I have seen a merman standing waist-deep in the ocean off my rock shore,

Unmistakably human and unmistakably a sea-beast: he submerged and never came up again,
While we stood watching. I do not know what he was, and I have no theory: but this was the least of wonders.

I have seen the United States grow up the strongest and wealthiest of nations, and swim in the wind over bankruptcy.
I have seen Europe, for twenty-five hundred years the crown of the world, become its beggar and cripple.

I have seen my people, fooled by ambitious men and a froth of sentiment, waste themselves on three wars.
None was required, all futile, all grandly victorious. A fourth is forming.

I have seen the invention of human flight; a chief desire of man's dreaming heart for ten thousand years;
And men have made it the chief of the means of massacre.

I have seen the far stars weighed and their distance measured, and the powers that make the atom put into service—
For what?—To kill. To kill half a million flies—men I should say—at one slap.

I have also seen doom. You can stand up and struggle or lie down and sleep—you are doomed as Oedipus.

A man and a civilization grow old, grow fatally—as we say—ill: courage and
the will are bystanders.

It is easy to know the beauty of inhuman things, sea, storm and mountain;
it is their soul and their meaning.
Humanity has its lesser beauty, impure and painful; we have to harden our
hearts to bear it.

I have hardened my heart only a little: I have learned that happiness is
important, but pain *gives* importance.
The use of tragedy: Lear becomes as tall as the storm he crawls in; and a
tortured Jew became God.

Edwin Muir

« 1887 – 1959 »

THE SUCCESSION

Legendary Abraham,
The old Chaldean wanderer,
First among these nations came,
Cruising above them like a star
That is in love with distances
And has through age to calmness grown,
Patient in the wilderness
And untarrying in the sown.
At last approached his setting mark.
Thence he sent his twin star out,
Isaac, to revolve alone.
For two great stars that through an age
Play in their corner of the sky
Separate go into the dark,
And ere they end their roundabout
One must live and one must die.

Isaac in his tutelage
Wheeled around the father light.
Then began his pilgrimage
Through another day and night,
Other peoples, other lands.
Where the father could not go
There is gone the careless son.
He can never miss his way.
By strangers' hands to strangers' hands
He is carried where he will.
Free, he must the powers obey,
Serve, be served by good and ill,

Safe through all the hazards run.
All shall watch him come and go
Until his quittance he has won;
And Jacob wheels into the day.

We through the generations came
Here by a way we do not know
From the fields of Abraham,
And still the road is scarce begun.
To hazard and to danger go
The sallying generations all
Where the imperial highways run.
And our songs and legends call
The hazard and the danger good;
For our fathers understood
That danger was by hope begot
And hazard by revolving chance
Since first we drew the enormous lot.

THE INCARNATE ONE

The windless northern surge, the sea-gull's scream,
And Calvin's kirk crowning the barren brae.
I think of Giotto the Tuscan shepherd's dream,
Christ, man and creature in their inner day.
How could our race betray
The Image, and the Incarnate One unmake
Who chose this form and fashion for our sake?

The Word made flesh here is made word again,
A word made word in flourish and arrogant crook.
See there King Calvin with iron pen,
And God three angry letters in a book,
And there the logical hook
On which the Mystery is impaled and bent
Into an ideological instrument.

There's better gospel in man's natural tongue,
And truer sight was theirs outside the Law
Who saw the far side of the Cross among
The archaic peoples in their ancient awe,
In ignorant wonder saw
The wooden cross-tree on the bare hillside,
Not knowing that there a God suffered and died.

The fleshless word, growing, will bring us down,
Pagan and Christian man alike will fall,
The auguries say, the white and black and brown,
The merry and sad, theorist, lover, all
Invisibly will fall:
Abstract calamity, save for those who can
Build their cold empire on the abstract man.

A soft breeze stirs and all my thoughts are blown
Far out to sea and lost. Yet I know well
The bloodless word will battle for its own
Invisibly in brain and nerve and cell.
The generations tell
Their personal tale: the One has far to go
Past the mirages and the murdering snow.

Marianne Moore

« 1887 – »

WHAT ARE YEARS?

What is our innocence,
what is our guilt? All are
naked, none is safe. And whence
is courage: the unanswered question,
the resolute doubt,—
dumbly calling, deafly listening—that
in misfortune, even death,
encourages others
and in its defeat, stirs

the soul to be strong? He
sees deep and is glad, who
accedes to mortality
and in his imprisonment rises
upon himself as
the sea in a chasm, struggling to be Prometheus
free and unable to be,
in its surrendering
finds its continuing.
So he who strongly feels,
behaves. The very bird,
grown taller as he sings, steels
his form straight up. Though he is captive,
his mighty singing
says, satisfaction is a lowly
thing, how pure a thing is joy.
This is mortality,
this is eternity.

Conrad Aiken

« 1889 – »

THE ROOM

Through that window—all else being extinct
Except itself and me—I saw the struggle
Of darkness against darkness. Within the room
It turned and turned, dived downward. Then I saw
How order might—if chaos wished—become:
And saw the darkness crush upon itself,
Contracting powerfully; it was as if
It killed itself: slowly: and with much pain.
Pain. The scene was pain, and nothing but pain.
What else, when chaos draws all forces inward
To shape a single leaf? . . .
For the leaf came,
Alone and shining in the empty room;
After a while the twig shot downward from it;
And from the twig a bough; and then the trunk,
Massive and coarse; and last the one black root.
The black root cracked the walls. Boughs burst the window:
The great tree took possession.
Tree of trees!
Remember (when time comes) how chaos died
To shape the shining leaf. Then turn, have courage,
Wrap arms and roots together, be convulsed
With grief, and bring back chaos out of shape.
I will be watching then as I watch now.
I will praise darkness now, but then the leaf.

SOUND OF BREAKING

Why do you cry out, why do I like to hear you
Cry out, here in the dewless evening, sitting
Close, close together, so close that the heart stops beating
And the brain its thought? Wordless, worthless mortals
Stumbling, exhausted, in this wilderness
Of our conjoint destruction! Hear the grass
Raging about us! Hear the worms applaud!
Hear how the ripples make a sound of chaos!
Hear now, in these and the other sounds of evening,
The first brute step of God!

About your elbow,
Making a ring of thumb and finger, I
Slide the walled blood against the less-walled blood,
Move down your arm, surmount the wrist-bone, shut
Your long slim hand in mine. Each finger-tip
Is then saluted by a finger-tip;
The hands meet back to back, then face to face;
Then lock together. And we, with eyes averted,
Smile at the evening sky of alabaster,
See nothing, lose our souls in the maelstrom, turning
Downward in rapid circles.

Bitter woman,
Bitter of heart and brain and blood, bitter as I
Who drink your bitterness—can this be beauty?
Do you cry out because the beauty is cruel?
Terror, because we downward sweep so swiftly?
Terror of darkness?

It is a sound of breaking,
The world is breaking, the world is a sound of breaking,
Many-harmonied, diverse, profound,
A shattering beauty. See, how together we break,
Hear what a crashing of disordered chords and discords
Fills the world with falling, when we thus lean
Our two mad bodies together!

It is a sound
Of everlasting grief, the sound of weeping,
The sound of disaster and misery, the sound
Of passionate heartbreak at the centre of the world.

e. e. cummings

« 1894 – 1962 »

WHEN ANY MORTAL (EVEN THE MOST ODD)

when any mortal (even the most odd)

can justify the ways of man to God
i'll think it strange that normal mortals can

not justify the ways of God to man.

Hart Crane

« 1899 - 1932 »

VOYAGES II

And yet this great wink of eternity,
Of rimless floods, unfettered leewardings,
Samite sheeted and processioned where
Her undinal vast belly moonward bends,
Laughing the wrapt inflections of our love;

Take this Sea, whose diapason knells
On scrolls of silver snowy sentences,
The sceptered terror of whose sessions rends
As her demeanors motion well or ill,
All but the pieties of lovers' hands.

And onward, as bells off San Salvador
Salute the crocus lustres of the stars,
In these poinsettia meadows of her tides,—
Adagios of islands, O my Prodigal,
Complete the dark confessions her veins spell.

Mark how her turning shoulders wind the hours,
And hasten while her penniless rich palms
Pass superscription of bent foam and wave,—
Hasten, while they are true,—sleep, death, desire,
Close round one instant in one floating flower.

Bind us in time, O Seasons clear, and awe.
O minstrel galleons of Carib fire,
Bequeath us to no earthly shore until
Is answered in the vortex of our grave
The seal's wide spindrift gaze toward paradise.

TO BROOKLYN BRIDGE (from "The Bridge")

How many dawns, chill from his rippling rest
The seagull's wings shall dip and pivot him,
Shedding white rings of tumult, building high
Over the chained bay waters Liberty—

Then, with inviolate curve, forsake our eyes
As apparitional as sails that cross
Some page of figures to be filed away;
—Till elevators drop us from our day . . .

I think of cinemas, panoramic sleights
With multitudes bent toward some flashing scene
Never disclosed, but hastened to again,
Foretold to other eyes on the same screen;

And Thee, across the harbor, silver-paced
As though the sun took step of thee, yet left
Some motion ever unspent in thy stride,—
Implicitly thy freedom staying thee!

Out of some subway scuttle, cell or loft
A bedlamite speeds to thy parapets,
Tilting there momently, shrill shirt ballooning,
A jest falls from the speechless caravan.

Down Wall, from girder into street noon leaks,
A rip-tooth of the sky's acetylene;
All afternoon the cloud-flown derricks turn . . .
Thy cables breathe the North Atlantic still.

And obscure as that heaven of the Jews,
Thy guerdon . . . Accolade thou dost bestow
Of anonymity time cannot raise:
Vibrant reprieve and pardon thou dost show.

O harp and altar, of the fury fused,
(How could mere toil align thy choiring strings!)
Terrific threshold of the prophet's pledge,
Prayer of pariah, and the lover's cry,—

Again the traffic lights that skim thy swift
Unfractioned idiom, immaculate sigh of stars,
Beading thy path—condense eternity:
And we have seen night lifted in thine arms.

Under thy shadow by the piers I waited;
Only in darkness is thy shadow clear.
The City's fiery parcels all undone,
Already snow submerges an iron year . . .

O Sleepless as the river under thee,
Vaulting the sea, the prairies' dreaming sod,
Unto us lowliest sometime sweep, descend
And of the curveship lend a myth to God.

Allen Tate

« 1899 – »

SONNETS AT CHRISTMAS

II

Ah, Christ, I love you rings to the wild sky
And I must think a little of the past:
When I was ten I told a stinking lie
That got a black boy whipped; but now at last
The going years, caught in an accurate glow,
Reverse like balls englished upon green baize—
Let them return, let the round trumpets blow
The ancient crackle of the Christ's deep gaze.

Deafened and blind, with senses yet unfound,
Am I, untutored to the after-wit
Of knowledge, knowing a nightmare has no sound;
Therefore with idle hands and head I sit
In late December before the fire's daze
Punished by crimes of which I would be quit.

Richard Eberhart

« 1904 – »

THE HORSE CHESTNUT TREE

Boys in sporadic but tenacious droves
Come with sticks, as certainly as Autumn,
To assault the great horse chestnut tree.

There is a law governs their lawlessness.
Desire is in them for a shining amulet
And the best are those that are highest up.

They will not pick them easily from the ground.
With shrill arms they fling to the higher branches,
To hurry the work of nature for their pleasure.

I have seen them trooping down the street
Their pockets stuffed with chestnuts shucked, unshucked.
It is only evening keeps them from their wish.

Sometimes I run out in a kind of rage
To chase the boys away; I catch an arm,
Maybe, and laugh to think of being the lawgiver.

I was once such a young sprout myself
And fingered in my pocket the prize and trophy.
But still I moralize upon the day

And see that we, outlaws on God's property,
Fling out imagination beyond the skies
Wishing a tangible good from the unknown.

And likewise death will drive us from the scene
With the great flowering world unbroken yet,
Which we held in idea, a little handful.

SEA SCAPE WITH PARABLE

A practical hand at catching fish is necessitous;
Mark the sociability, as in the fish themselves
Who dance, pronounce, waltz, or as it were rollick
In close presses of their solidarity toward Weir Cove,
A natural phenomenon. God, I suppose, sends them.
And the fishers, drawn from hamlet, farm, and dock,
Push out their various vessels and elenctic gear,
At a sign come quickly to the holy mackerel.

These are dancing on the water, with professional ease.
Are cast prophetic nets, with a glance cast at the weather.
Jubilation sits in the eyes of old and young: a catch.
It is as yare as anything in the book of sea lore,
The time right, wind and wave crucially conspiring.
The gulls, above, pervade the sky; far off the ospreys
Sit meanly on their rocks, barbarous, meditative.
It is an event social, of bulging, conclamant waters,
An exercise in a precise corner of the right sea.

It is not to speak of ghostly scavengers,
Not in the sky can be seen absolute integers
To the contemplative sense: oilskinned men
Traverse a shining field of water like toed dancers;
Time the skilled fisherman they do not see,
Nor feel their bones consecrated to the rocky walls,
Nor flesh reduced by rough force to everlasting lightness.

The work goes on as it always has; some hours of sun
And wind, and jockeyings of the ropes, calculations
Of stress, a lively timing, expert arraignment
Of the mass, and finally the huge haul comes in.

The shining victims, lost multitudinously
Are hoisted and shovelled into the capacious holds.
  As silently as fish are vigorously together
  Swimming, directed by the laws that govern them,
  Who come this time of year to this defeating place,
  The fishermen veer off and fall away at eventide,
  Rich with big increase, leaving a vacant sea.
  Which, seen in retrospect, as if without event,
  Is full of a wide and charming serenity.

So by the inevitable analogy, are fished
Souls by the Fisher King, who with the net of time
Searches them into the silent bin of death,
Yet ever vigorous swarms of men laugh with the living.

It is true that sometimes, due to some error in man,
Some clumsy misadventure, the whole lot gets away,
And he goes back to land without his edibles,
Mocked, disenchanted, hugging his big stupidity,
Awaiting another try at the fabulous oncome.

Yet who would say, in all philosophy,
That the Master of Mankind errs and is vain?
Who would disallow the Fisher's victory,
As we drink our spirit in the haven halls of men?

Robert Penn Warren

« 1905 – »

DARK WOODS

– II. THE DOGWOOD –

All right: and with that wry acceptance you follow the cow-track.
Yes, it's dark in the woods, as black as a peddler's pocket.
Cobweb tangles, briar snatches. A sensible man would go back.
A bough finds your face, and one eye grieves in the socket.

Midnight compounds with the peeper. Now whippoorwills speak,
Far off. Then silence. What's that? And something blots star—
By your head velvet air-*whoosh*, curdle and shudder of wing-creak.
It is only an owl. You go on. You can guess where you are.

For here is the gum-swamp, the slough where you once trapped the weasel.
Here the dead cow was dumped, and by buzzards duly divested.
All taint of mortality's long since wiped clean as a whistle.
Now love vine threads eyehole, God's peace is by violet attested.

The bones are long lost. In green grass the skull waits, has waited:
A cathedral for ants, and at noon, under white dome, great transept,
They pass in green gloom, under sunlight by leaf mitigated,
For leaf of the love vine shuts eyehole, as though the eye slept.

But now it's not noon, it is night, and ant-dark in that cow skull.
And man-dark in the woods. But go on, that's how men survive.
Went on in the dark, heart tight now as nut in the hull.
Came back in the dark, and home, and throve as men thrive.

But not before you had seen it, sudden at path-turn,
White-floating in darkness, the dogwood, white bloom in dark air.

Like an ice-break, broke joy; then you felt a strange wrath burn
To strike it, and strike, had a stick been handy in the dark there.

But one wasn't handy, so there on the path now, breath scant,
You stood, you stood there, and oh, could the poor heart's absurd
Cry for wisdom, for wisdom, ever be answered? Triumphant,
All night, the tree glimmered in darkness, and uttered no word.

W. H. Auden

« 1907 – »

SEXT (from "Horae Canonicae")

– 1 –

You need not see what someone is doing
to know if it is his vocation,

you have only to watch his eyes:
a cook mixing a sauce, a surgeon

making a primary incision,
a clerk completing a bill of lading,

wear the same rapt expression,
forgetting themselves in a function.

How beautiful it is,
that eye-on-the-object look.

To ignore the appetitive goddesses,
to desert the formidable shrines

of Rhea, Aphrodite, Demeter, Diana,
to pray instead to St. Phocas,

St. Barbara, San Saturnino,
or whoever one's patron is,

that one may be worthy of their mystery,
what a prodigious step to have taken.

There should be monuments, there should be odes,
to the nameless heroes who took it first,

to the first flaker of flints
who forgot his dinner,

the first collector of sea-shells
to remain celibate.

Where should we be but for them?
Feral still, un-housetrained, still

wandering through forests without
a consonant to our names,

slaves of Dame Kind, lacking
all notion of a city

and, at this noon, for this death,
there would be no agents.

– 2 –

You need not hear what orders he is giving
to know if someone has authority,

you have only to watch his mouth:
when a besieging general sees

a city wall breached by his troops,
when a bacteriologist

realizes in a flash what was wrong
with his hypothesis, when,

from a glance at the jury, the prosecutor
knows the defendant will hang,

their lips and the lines around them
relax, assuming an expression,

not of simple pleasure at getting
their own sweet way but of satisfaction

of being right, an incarnation
of *Fortitudo, Justicia, Nous.*

You may not like them much
(Who does?) but we owe them

basilicas, divas,
dictionaries, pastoral verse,

the courtesies of the city:
without these judicial mouths

(which belong for the most part
to very great scoundrels)

how squalid existence would be,
tethered for life to some hut village,

afraid of the local snake
or the local ford demon,

speaking the local patois
of some three hundred words

(think of the family squabbles and the
poison-pens, think of the inbreeding)

and, at this noon, there would be no authority
to command this death.

– 3 –

Anywhere you like, somewhere
on broad-chested life-giving Earth,

anywhere between her thirstlands
and undrinkable Ocean,

the crowd stands perfectly still,
its eyes (which seem one) and its mouths

(which seem infinitely many)
expressionless, perfectly blank.

The crowd does not see (what everyone sees)
a boxing match, a train wreck,

a battleship being launched,
does not wonder (as everyone wonders)

who will win, what flag she will fly,
how many will be burned alive,

is never distracted
(as everyone is always distracted)

by a barking dog, a smell of fish,
a mosquito on a bald head:

the crowd sees only one thing
(which only the crowd can see),

an epiphany of that
which does whatever is done.

Whatever god a person believes in,
in whatever way he believes

(no two are exactly alike),
as one of the crowd he believes

and only believes in that
in which there is only one way of believing.

Few people accept each other and most
will never do anything properly,

but the crowd rejects no one, joining the crowd
is the only thing all men can do.

Only because of that can we say
all men are our brothers,

superior, because of that,
to the social exoskeletons: When

have they ever ignored their queens,
for one second stopped work

on their provincial cities, to worship
The Prince of this world like us,

at this noon, on this hill,
in the occasion of this dying.

Louis MacNeice

« 1907 – 1963 »

HANDS AND EYES

In a high wind
Gnarled hands cup to kindle an old briar,
From a frilled cot
Twin sea anemones grope for a hanging lamp,
In a foul cage
Old coal-gloves dangle from dejected arms.

Of which three pairs of hands the child's are helpless
(Whose wheels barely engage)
And the shepherd's from his age are almost bloodless
While the chimpanzee's are hopeless
Were there not even a cage.

In a dark room
Docile pupils grow to their full prey,
Down a long bar
Mascara scraws a gloss on a torn leaf,
On a high col
The climber's blue marries the blue he climbs.

Of which three pairs of eyes the tart's are mindless
(Who pawned her mind elsewhere)
And the black cat's, in gear with black, are heartless
While the alpinist's are timeless
In gear with timeless air.

In a cold church
It flickers in the draught, then burns erect;
In a loud mob

It bulges, merges, feels with a start alone;
In a bright beam
It waltzes dust to dust with its chance loves.

Of which three souls the praying one is selfless
But only for a span
And the gregarious man's is rudderless, powerless,
While the soul in love is luckless,
Betrays what chance it can.

And still the wind
Blows, the ape is marooned, the lamp ungrasped;
Woman and cat
Still wait to pounce and the climber waits to fall;
As each soul burns
The best it may, in foul or blustering air.
Oh would He, were there a God, have mercy on us all?

Elizabeth Bishop

« 1911 – »

OVER 2000 ILLUSTRATIONS AND A COMPLETE CONCORDANCE

Thus should have been our travels:
serious, engravable.
The Seven Wonders of the World are tired
and a touch familiar, but the other scenes,
innumerable, though equally sad and still,
are foreign. Often the squatting Arab,
or group of Arabs, plotting, probably,
against our Christian Empire,
while one apart, with outstretched arm and hand
points to the Tomb, the Pit, the Sepulcher.
The branches of the date-palms look like files.
The cobbled courtyard, where the Well is dry,
is like a diagram, the brickwork conduits
are vast and obvious, the human figure
far gone in history or theology,
gone with its camel or its faithful horse.
Always the silence, the gesture, the specks of birds
suspended on invisible threads above the Site,
or the smoke rising solemnly, pulled by threads.
Granted a page alone or a page made up
of several scenes arranged in cattycornered rectangles
or circles set on stippled gray,
granted a grim lunette,
caught in the toils of an initial letter,
when dwelt upon, they all resolve themselves.
The eye drops, weighted, through the lines
the burin made, the lines that move apart
like ripples above sand,

dispersing storms, God's spreading fingerprint,
and painfully, finally, that ignite
in watery prismatic white-and-blue.

Entering the Narrows at St. Johns
the touching bleat of goats reached to the ship.
We glimpsed them, reddish, leaping up the cliffs
among the fog-soaked weeds and butter-and-eggs.
And at St. Peter's the wind blew and the sun shone madly.
Rapidly, purposefully, the Collegians marched in lines,
crisscrossing the great square with black, like ants.
In Mexico the dead man lay
in a blue arcade; the dead volcanoes
glistened like Easter lilies.
The juke-box went on playing "Ay, Jalisco!"
And at Volubilis there were beautiful poppies
splitting the mosaics; the fat old guide made eyes.
In Dingle harbor a golden length of evening
the rotting hulks held up their dripping plush.
The Englishwoman poured tea, informing us
that the Duchess was going to have a baby.
And in the brothels of Marrakesh
the little pockmarked prostitutes
balanced their tea-trays on their heads
and did their belly-dances; flung themselves
naked and giggling against our knees,
asking for cigarettes. It was somewhere near there
I saw what frightened me most of all:
A holy grave, not looking particularly holy,
one of a group under a keyhole-arched stone baldaquin
open to every wind from the pink desert.
An open, gritty, marble trough, carved solid
with exhortation, yellowed
as scattered cattle-teeth;
half-filled with dust, not even the dust
of the poor prophet paynim who once lay there.
In a smart burnoose Khadour looked on amused.

Everything only connected by "and," and "and."
Open the book. (The gilt rubs off the edges
of the pages and pollinates the fingertips.)

Open the heavy book. Why couldn't we have seen
this old Nativity while we were at it?
—the dark ajar, the rocks breaking with light,
an undisturbed, unbreathing flame,
colorless, sparkless, freely fed on straw,
and, lulled within, a family with pets,
—and looked and looked our infant sight away.

Delmore Schwartz

« 1913 – »

IN THE NAKED BED, IN PLATO'S CAVE

In the naked bed, in Plato's cave,
Reflected headlights slowly slid the wall,
Carpenters hammered under the shaded window,
Wind troubled the window curtains all night long.
A fleet of trucks strained uphill, grinding,
Their freights covered, as usual.
The ceiling lightened again, the slanting diagram
Slid slowly forth.
Hearing the milkman's chop,
His striving up the stair, the bottle's chink,
I rose from bed, lit a cigarette,
And walked to the window. The stony street
Displayed the stillness in which buildings stand,
The street-lamp's vigil and the horse's patience.
The winter sky's pure capital
Turned me back to bed with exhausted eyes.
Strangeness grew in the motionless air. The loose
Film grayed. Shaking wagons, hooves' waterfalls,
Sounded far off, increasing, louder and nearer.
A car coughed, starting. Morning, softly
Melting the air, lifted the half-covered chair
From underseas, kindled the looking-glass,
Distinguished the dresser and the white wall.
The bird called tentatively, whistled, called,
Bubbled and whistled, so! Perplexed, still wet
With sleep, affectionate, hungry and cold. So, so,
O son of man, the ignorant night, the travail
Of early morning, the mystery of beginning
Again and again,
while History is unforgiven.

THE STARLIGHT'S INTUITIONS PIERCED THE TWELVE

The starlight's intuitions pierced the twelve,
The brittle night sky sparkled like a tune
Tinkled and tapped out on the xylophone.
Empty and vain, a glittering dune, the moon
Arose too big, and, in the mood which ruled,
Seemed like a useless beauty in a pit;
And then one said, after he carefully spat:
'No matter what we do, he looks at it!

'I cannot see a child or find a girl
Beyond his smile which glows like that spring moon.'
'—Nothing no more the same,' the second said,
'Though all may be forgiven, never quite healed
The wound I bear as witness, standing by;
No ceremony surely appropriate,
Nor secret love, escape or sleep because
No matter what I do, he looks at it—'

'Now,' said the third, 'no thing will be the same:
I am as one who never shuts his eyes,
The sea and sky no more are marvellous,
And I no longer understand surprise!'
'Now,' said the fourth, 'nothing will be enough
—I heard his voice accomplishing all wit:
No word can be unsaid, no deed withdrawn
—No matter what is said, he measures it!'

'Vision, imagination, hope or dream
Believed, denied, the scene we wished to see?
It does not matter in the least: for what
Is altered, if it is not true? That we
Saw goodness, as it is—*this* is the awe
And the abyss which we will not forget,
His story now the sky which holds all thought:
No matter what I think, think of it!'

'And I will never be what once I was,'
Said one for long as narrow as a knife,
'And we will never be what once we were;
We have died once; this is a second life.'
'My mind is spilled in moral chaos,' one
Righteous as Job exclaimed, 'now infinite
Suspicion of my heart stems what I will
—No matter what I choose, he stares at it!'

'I am as one native in summer places
—Ten weeks' excitement paid for by the rich;
Debauched by that and then all winter bored,'
The sixth declared. 'His peak left us a ditch!'
'He came to make this life more difficult,'
The seventh said, 'No one will ever fit
His measures' heights, all is inadequate:
No matter what I do, what good is it?'

'He gave forgiveness to us: what a gift!'
The eighth chimed in. 'But now we know how much
Must be forgiven. But if forgiven, what?
The crime which was will be; and the least touch
Revives the memory: what is forgiveness worth?'
The ninth spoke thus: 'Who now will ever sit
At ease in Zion at the Easter feast?
No matter what the place, he touches it!'

'And I will always stammer, since he spoke,'
One, who had been most eloquent, said, stammering.
'I looked too long at the sun; like too much light,
So too much of goodness is a boomerang,'
Laughed the eleventh of the troop. 'I must
Try what he tried: I saw the infinite
Who walked the lake and raised the hopeless dead:
No matter what the feat, he first accomplished it!'

So spoke the twelfth; and then the twelve in chorus:
'Unspeakable unnatural goodness is
Risen and shines, and never will ignore us;
He glows forever in all consciousness;
Forgiveness, love, and hope possess the pit,
And bring our endless guilt, like shadow's bars:

No matter what we do, he stares at it!
What pity then deny? What debt defer?
We know he looks at us like all the stars,
And we shall never be as once we were,
This life will never be what once it was!'

Cecil Hemley

« 1914 – »

WITNESSES

Once quiet meant discord and pain;
My frantic mind willed hurricane
To blow away its disbelief,
But violence brought it no relief.
How does it happen that a bough
In winter stillness calms me now?

The spirit sees what it has known;
It prints its trials on leaf and stone.
So leaf and stone record for me
The ways I went unwittingly.
What did I find? What do I know
That makes the silence beckon so?

Howard Nemerov

« 1920 – »

MOMENT

Now, starflake frozen on the windowpane
All of a winter night, the open hearth
Blazing beyond Andromeda, the sea—
Anemone and the downwind seed, O moment
Hastening, halting in a clockwise dust,
The time in all the hospitals is now,
Under the arc-lights where the sentry walks
His lonely wall it never moves from now,
The crying in the cell is also now,
And now is quiet in the tomb as now
Explodes inside the sun, and it is now
In the saddle of space, where argosies of dust
Sail outward blazing, and the mind of God,
The flash across the gap of being, thinks
In the instant absence of forever: now.

BOOM!

SEES BOOM IN RELIGION, TOO

> *Atlantic City, June 23, 1957 (AP).—President Eisenhower's pastor said tonight that Americans are living in a period of "unprecedented religious activity" caused partially by paid vacations, the eight-hour day and modern conveniences.*
>
> *"These fruits of material progress," said the Rev. Edward L. R. Elson of the National Presbyterian Church, Washington, "have provided the leisure, the energy, and the means for a level of human and spiritual values never before reached."*

Here at the Vespasian-Carlton, it's just one
religious activity after another; the sky
is constantly being crossed by cruciform
airplanes, in which nobody disbelieves
for a second, and the tide, the tide
of spiritual progress and prosperity
miraculously keeps rising, to a level
never before attained. The churches are full,
the beaches are full, and the filling-stations
are full, God's great ocean is full
of paid vacationers praying an eight-hour day
to the human and spiritual values, the fruits,
the leisure, the energy, and the means, Lord,
the means for the level, the unprecedented level,
and the modern conveniences, which also are full.
Never before, O Lord, have the prayers and praises
from belfry and phonebooth, from ballpark and barbecue
the sacrifices, so endlessly ascended.

It was not thus when Job in Palestine
sat in the dust and cried, cried bitterly;
when Damien kissed the lepers on their wounds
it was not thus; it was not thus
when Francis worked a fourteen-hour day
strictly for the birds; when Dante took
a week's vacation without pay and it rained
part of the time, O Lord, it was not thus.

But now the gears mesh and the tires burn
and the ice chatters in the shaker and the priest
in the pulpit, and Thy Name, O Lord,
is kept before the public, while the fruits
ripen and religion booms and the level rises
and every modern convenience runneth over,
that it may never be with us as it hath been
with Athens and Karnak and Nagasaki,
nor Thy sun for one instant refrain from shining
on the rainbow Buick by the breezeway
or the Chris Craft with the uplift life raft;
that we may continue to be the just folks we are,
plain people with ordinary superliners and
disposable diaperliners, people of the stop'n'shop
'n'pray as you go, of hotel, motel, boatel,
the humble pilgrims of no deposit no return
and please adjust thy clothing, who will give to Thee,
if Thee will keep us going, our annual
Miss Universe, for Thy Name's Sake, Amen.

Richard Wilbur

« 1921 – »

FOR THE NEW RAILWAY STATION IN ROME

Those who said God is praised
By hurt pillars, who loved to see our brazen lust
Lie down in rubble, and our vaunting arches
Conduce to dust;

Those who with short shadows
Poked through the stubbled forum pondering on decline,
And would not take the sun standing at noon
For a good sign;

Those pilgrims of defeat
Who brought their injured wills as to a soldiers' home;
Dig them all up now, tell them there's something new
To see in Rome.

See, from the travertine
Face of the office block, the roof of the booking-hall
Sails out into the air beside the ruined
Servian Wall,

Echoing in its light
And cantilevered swoop of reinforced concrete
The broken profile of these stones, defeating
That defeat

And straying the strummed mind,
By such a sudden chord as raised the town of Troy,
To where the least shard of the world sings out
In stubborn joy,

"What city is eternal
But that which prints itself within the groping head
Out of the blue unbroken reveries
Of the building dead?

"What is our praise or pride
But to imagine excellence, and try to make it?
What does it say over the door of Heaven
But *homo fecit?*"

Gene Baro

« 1924 – »

SEBASTIAN

For Clyde Miller

– I –

Focus of eyes, focus of arrows:
This is the plot the body demanded,
young captain and hero.
To turn upon the spiritual,
the logic of flesh is first dumbfounded
by metaphysicals.

What was surrendered was first the source,
a plenitude of the self extended
as far as its reverse.

The body conceived as lyrical
meaning is only by death augmented,
makes pain its miracle.

There was this wild flight of tenderness
outward and inward; arrows invaded
ultimate nakedness.

– II –

It must be made simple, free of regret,
that the saint speaks out of the untried flesh,
the young flesh telling of the reasoned death.

From such logic is life made accurate,
and joy possesses the mean raw spirit
that suddenly speaks in a golden breath.

Innocence is in this without merit,
when the cohort from the hail of arrows
returns to argue his logical death.

The hero is in this most passionate
and knowledgeable, arrows and iron lash
being but the poor flesh made manifest.

Mastery of the violent spirit
demands the passion of accurate flesh,
extinction! o bowman, o target!

– III –

God made sweet, meek, and militant
Christ's rough young captain, but, after,
what was he under arrogant
flails? Less did Caesar's cold laughter
deny him than Christ adamant.
In the travail for God's kingdom,
there can be but one marytrdom.

But more martyrs are arguments
profoundly in holy service,
that creating of innocents
and innocence of God's purpose.
Who fear death lie in violence,
for that old wound is viable
as young flesh in its miracle.

Godhead is source, and hesitant
how power is given; lest love
embrace heaven, flesh is dissonant
and the mind seeks to prove and prove.
Yet of all this the increment
is death; the gift but an infant
corruptible and triumphant.

Elizabeth Jennings

« 1926 –   »

ANSWERS

I kept my answers small and kept them near;
Big questions bruised my mind but still I let
Small answers be a bulwark to my fear.

The huge abstractions I kept from the light;
Small things I handled and caressed and loved.
I let the stars assume the whole of night.

But the big answers clamoured to be moved
Into my life. Their great audacity
Shouted to be acknowledged and believed.

Even when all small answers build up to
Protection of my spirit, still I hear
Big answers striving for their overthrow

And all the great conclusions coming near.

Galway Kinnell

« 1927 –   »

THE AVENUE BEARING THE INITIAL OF CHRIST INTO THE NEW WORLD

Was diese kleine Gasse doch für ein Reich an sich war . . .

For Gail

– 1 –

pcheek pcheek pcheek pcheek pcheek
They cry. The motherbirds thieve the air
To appease them. A tug on the East River
Blasts the bass-note of its passage, lifted
From the infra-bass of the sea. A broom
Swishes over the sidewalk like feet through leaves.
Valerio's pushcart Ice Coal Kerosene
Moves   clack
                        clack
                                    clack
On a broken wheelrim. Ringing in its chains
The New Star Laundry horse comes down the street
Like a roofleak whucking in a pail.
At the redlight, where a horn blares,
The Golden Harvest Bakery brakes on its gears,
Squeaks, and seethes in place. A propane-
gassed bus makes its way with big, airy sighs.

Across the street a woman throws open
Her window,
She sets, terribly softly,

Two potted plants on the windowledge
tic tic
And bangs shut her window.
A man leaves a doorway tic toc tic toc tic toc tic hurrah
toc splat on Avenue C tic etc and turns the corner.

Banking the same corner
A pigeon coasts 5th Street in shadows,
Looks for altitude, surmounts the rims of buildings,
And turns white.

The babybirds pipe down. It is day.

– 2 –

In sunlight on the Avenue
The Jew rocks along in a black fur shtraimel,
Black robe, black knickers, black knee-stockings,
Black shoes. His beard like a sod-bottom
Hides the place where he wears no tie.
A dozen children troop after him, barbels flying,
In skullcaps. They are Reuben, Simeon, Levi, Judah, Issachar, Zebulun,
Benjamin, Dan, Naphtali, Gad, Asher.
With the help of the Lord they will one day become
Courtiers, thugs, rulers, rabbis, asses, adders, wrestlers, bakers, poets, cart-
pushers, infantrymen.

The old man is sad-faced. He is near burial
And one son is missing. The women who bore him sons
And are past bearing, mourn for the son
And for the father, wondering if the man will go down
Into the grave of a son mourning, or if at the last
The son will put his hands on the eyes of his father.

The old man wades towards his last hour.
On 5th Street, between Avenues A and B,
In sunshine, in his private cloud, Bunko Certified Embalmer,
Cigar in his mouth, nose to the wind, leans
At the doorway of Bunko's Funeral Home & Parlour,
Glancing west towards the Ukrainians, eastward idly
Where the Jew rocks towards his last hour.

Sons, grandsons at his heel, the old man
Confronts the sun. He does not feel its rays
Through his beard, he does not understand
Fruits and vegetables live by the sun.
Like his children he is sallow-faced, he sees
A blinding signal in the sky, he smiles.

Bury me not Bunko damned Catholic I pray you in Egypt.

– 3 –

From the Station House
Under demolishment on Houston
To the Power Station on 14th,
Jews, Negroes, Puerto Ricans
Walk in the spring sunlight.

The Downtown Talmud Torah
Blosztein's Cutrate Bakery
Areceba Panataria Hispano
Peanuts Dried Fruit Nuts & Canned Goods
Productos Tropicales
Appetizing Herring Candies Nuts
Nathan Kugler Chicken Store Fresh Killed Daily
Little Rose Restaurant
Rubinstein the Hatter Mens Boys Hats Caps Furnishings
J. Herrmann Dealer in All Kinds of Bottles
Natural Bloom Cigars
Blony Bubblegum
Mueren las Cucarachas Super Potente Garantizada de Matar las Cucarachas
mas Resistentes
Wenig מצבות
G. Schnee Stairbuilder
Everyouth la Original Loción Eterna Juventud Satisfacción Dinero Devuelto
Happy Days Bar & Grill

Through dust-stained windows over storefronts
Curtains drawn aside, onto the Avenue
Thronged with Puerto Ricans, Negroes, Jews,
Baby carriages stuffed with groceries and babies,
The old women peer, blessed damozels

Sitting up there young forever in the cockroached rooms,
Eating fresh-killed chicken, productos tropicales,
Appetizing herring, canned goods, nuts;
They puff out smoke from Natural Bloom cigars
And one day they puff like Blony Bubblegum.
Across the square skies with faces in them
Pigeons skid, crashing into the brick.
From a rooftop a boy fishes at the sky,
Around him a flock of pigeons fountains,
Blown down and swirling up again, seeking the sky.
From a skyview of the city they must seem
A whirlwind on the desert seeking itself;
Here they break from the rims of the buildings
Without rank in the blue military cemetery sky.
A red kite wriggles like a tadpole
Into the sky beyond them, crosses
The sun, lays bare its own crossed skeleton.

To fly from this place—to roll
On some bubbly blacktop in the summer,
To run under the rain of pigeon plumes, to be
Tarred, and feathered with birdshit, Icarus,

In Kugler's glass headdown dangling by yellow legs.

– 4 –

First Sun Day of the year. Tonight,
When the sun will have turned from the earth,
She will appear outside Hy's Luncheonette,
The crone who sells the *News* and the *Mirror,*
The oldest living thing on Avenue C,
Outdating much of its brick and mortar.
If you ask for the *News* she gives you the *Mirror*
And squints long at the nickel in her hand
Despising it, perhaps, for being a nickel,
And stuffs it in her apron pocket
And sucks her lips. Rain or stars, every night
She is there, squatting on the orange crate,
Issuing out only in darkness, like the cucarachas
And strange nightmares in the chambers overhead.

She can't tell one newspaper from another,
She has forgotten how Nain her dead husband looked,
She has forgotten her children's whereabouts
Or how many there were, or what the *News*
And *Mirror* tell about that we buy them with nickels.
She is sure only of the look of a nickel
And that there is a Lord in the sky overhead.
She dwells in a flesh that is of the Lord
And drifts out, therefore, only in darkness
Like the streetlamp outside the Luncheonette
Or the lights in the secret chamber
In the firmament, where Yahweh himself dwells.
Like Magdelene in the Battistero of Saint John
On the carved-up continent, in the land of sun,
She lives shadowed, under a feeble bulb
That lights her face, her crab's hands, her small bulk on the crate.

She is Pulchería mother of murderers and madmen,
She is also Alyona whose neck was a chicken leg.

Mother was it the insufferable wind?
She sucks her lips a little further into the mousehole.
She stares among the stars, and among the streetlamps.

The mystery is hers.

– 5 –

That violent song of the twilight!
Now, in the silence, will the motherbirds
Be dead, and the infantbirds
That were in the dawn merely transparent
Unfinished things, nothing but bellies,
Will they have been shoved out
And in the course of a morning, casually,
On scrawny wings, have taken up the life?

– 6 –

In the pushcart market, on Sunday,
A crate of lemons discharges light like a battery.
Icicle-shaped carrots that through black soil

Wove away lie like flames in the sun.
Onions with their shirts ripped seek sunlight
On green skins. The sun beats
On beets dirty as boulders in cowfields,
On turnips pinched and gibbous
From budging rocks, on embery sweets,
Peanut-shaped Idahos, shore-pebble Long Islands and Maines,
On horseradishes still growing weeds on the flat ends,
Cabbages lying about like sea-green brains
The skulls have been shucked from,
On tomatoes, undented plum-tomatoes, alligator-skinned
Cucumbers, that float pickled
In the wooden tubs of green skim milk—

Sky-flowers, dirt-flowers, underdirt-flowers,
Those that climbed for the sun in their lives
And those that wormed away—equally uprooted,
Maimed, lopped, shucked, and misaimed.

In the market in Damascus a goat
Came to a stall where twelve goatheads
Were lined up for sale. It sniffed them
One by one. Finally thirteen goats started
Smiling in their faintly sardonic way.

A crone buys a pickle from a crone,
It is wrapped in the *Mirror,*
At home she will open the wrapping, stained,
And stare and stare and stare at it.
And the cucumbers, and the melons,
And the leeks, and the onions, and the garlic.

– 7 –

Already the Avenue troughs the light of day.
Southwards, towards Houston and Pitt,
Where Avenue C begins, the eastern ranges
Of the wiped-out lives—punks, lushes,
Panhandlers, pushers, rumsoaks, everyone
Who took it easy when he should have been out failing at something—
The pots-and-pans man pushes his cart,

Through the intersection of the light, at 3rd,
Where sunset smashes on the aluminum of it,
On the bottoms, curves, handles, metal panes,
Mirrors: of the bead-curtained cave under the falls
In Freedom, Seekonk Woods leafing the light out,
Halfway to Kingston where a road branches out suddenly,
Between Pamplonne and Les Salins two meeting paths
Over a sea the green of churchsteeple copper.
Of all places on earth inhabited by men
Why is it we find ourselves on this Avenue
Where the dusk gets worse,
And the mirrorman pushing his heaped mirrors
Into the shadows between 3rd and 2nd,
Pushes away a mess of old pots and pans?

The ancient Negro sits as usual
Outside the Happy Days Bar & Grill. He wears
Dark glasses. Every once in a while, abruptly,
He starts to sing, chanting in a hoarse, nearly breaking
Voice—

ooooooooooooo v u h u h   jawwwwwww w w w w din

And becomes silent
Stares into the polaroid Wilderness
Gross-Rosen, Maidanek, Flössenberg, Ravensbruck, Stutthof, Riga, Bergen-Belsen, Mauthausen, Birkenau, Treblinka, Natzweiler, Dachau, Buchenwald, Auschwitz—
Villages,
Pasture-bordered hamlets on the far side of the river.

– 8 –

The promise was broken too freely
To them and to their fathers, for them to care.
They survive like cedars on a cliff, roots
Hooked in any crevice they can find.
They walk Avenue C in shadows
Neither conciliating its Baalim
Nor whoring after landscapes of the senses,

Tarig bab el Amoud being in the blood
Fumigated by Puerto Rican cooking.

Among women girthed like cedar trees
Other, slenderer ones appear:
One yellow haired, in August,
Under shooting stars on the lake, who
Believed in promises which broke by themselves—
In a German flower garden in the Bronx
The wedding of a child and a child, one flesh
Divided in the Adirondack spring—
One who found in the desert city of the West
The first happiness, and fled therefore—
And by a southern sea, in the pines, one loved
Until the mist rose blue in the trees
Around the spiderwebs that kept on shining,
Each day of the shortening summer.

And as rubbish burns
And the pushcarts are loaded
With fruit and vegetables and empty crates
And clank away on iron wheels over cobblestones,
And merchants infold their stores
And the carp ride motionlessly sleeplessly
In the dark tank in the fishmarket,
The figures withdraw into chambers overhead—
In the city of the mind, chambers built
Of care and necessity, where, hands lifted to the blinds,
They glimpse in mirrors backed with the blackness of the world
Awkward, cherished rooms containing the familiar selves.

– 9 –

Children set fires in ashbarrels,
Cats prowl the fires, scraps of fishes burn.

A child lay in the flames.
It was not the plan. Abraham
Stood in terror at the duplicity.
Isaac whom he loved lay in the flames.
The Lord turned away washing

His hands without soap and water
Like a common housefly.

The children laugh.
Isaac means *he laughs.*
Maybe the last instant,
The dying itself, *is* easier,
Easier anyway than the hike
From Pitt the blind gut
To the East River of Fishes,
Maybe it is as the poet said,
And the soul turns to thee
O vast and well-veiled Death
And the body gratefully nestles close to thee—

I think of Isaac reading Whitman in Chicago,
The week before he died, coming across
Such a passage and muttering, Oi!
What shit! And smiling, but not for you—I mean,

For *thee,* Sane and Sacred Death!

– 10 –

It was Gold's junkhouse, the one the clacking
Carts that little men pad after in harnesses
Picking up bedbugged mattresses, springs
The stubbornness has been loved out of,
Chairs felled by fat, lampshades lights have burned through,
Linoleum the geometry has been scuffed from,
Carriages a single woman's work has brought to wreck,
Would come to in the dusk and unload before,
That the whole neighborhood came out to see
Burning in the night, flames opening out like
Eyelashes from the windows, men firing the tears in,
Searchlights coming on like streams of water, smashing
On the brick, the water blooming up the wall
Like pale trees, reaching into the darkness beyond.

Nobody mourned, nobody stood around in pajamas
And a borrowed coat steaming his nose in coffee.

It was only Gold's junkhouse.
                                                  But this evening
The neighborhood comes out again, everything
That may abide the fire was made to go through the fire
And it was made clean: a few twisted springs,
Charred mattresses (crawling still, naturally),
Perambulator skeletons, bicycles tied in knots—
In a great black pile at the junkhouse door,
Smelling of burnt rubber and hair. Rustwater
Hangs in icicles over the windows and door,
Like frozen piss aimed at trespassers,
Combed by wind, set overnight. Carriages we were babies in,
Springs that used to resist love, that gave in
And were thrown out like whores—the black
Irreducible heap, mausoleum of what we were—
It is cold suddenly, we feel chilled,
Nobody knows for sure what is left of him.

– II –

The fishmarket closed, the fishes gone into flesh.
The smelts draped on each other, fat with roe,
The marble cod hacked into chunks on the counter,
Butterfishes mouths still open, still trying to eat,
Porgies with receding jaws hinged apart
In a grimace of dejection, as if like cows
They had died under the sledgehammer, perches
In grass-green armor, spotted squeteagues
In the melting ice meek-faced and croaking no more,
Except in the plip plop plip plip in the bucket,
Mud-eating mullets buried in crushed ice,
Tilefishes with scales like chickenfat,
Spanish mackerels, buttercups on the flanks,
Pot-bellied pikes, two-tone flounders
After the long contortion of pushing both eyes
To the brown side that they might look up,
Brown side down, like a mass laying-on of hands,
Or the oath-taking of an army.

The only things alive are the carp
That drift in the black tank in the rear,

Kept living for the usual reason, that they have not died,
And perhaps because the last meal was garbage and they might begin stink-
ing
On dying, before the customer was halfway home.
They nudge each other, to be netted,
The sweet flesh to be lifted thrashing in the air,
To be slugged, and then to keep on living
While they are opened on the counter.
Fishes do not die exactly, it is more
That they go out of themselves, the visible part
Remains the same, there is little pallor,
Only the cataracted eyes which have not shut ever
Must look through the mist which crazed Homer.

These are the vegetables of the deep,
The Sheol-flowers of darkness, swimmers
Of denser darknesses where the sun's rays bend for the last time
And in the sky there burns this shifty jellyfish
That degenerates and flashes and re-forms.

Motes in the eye land is the lid of,
They are plucked out of the green skim milk of the eye.

Fishes are nailed on the wood,
The big Jew stands like Christ, nailing them to the wood,
He scrapes the knife up the grain, the scales fly,
He unnails them, reverses them, nails them again,
Scrapes and the scales fly. He lops off the heads,
Shakes out the guts as if they did not belong in the first place,
And they are flesh for the first time in their lives.

Dear Frau ____________ :

Your husband, ____________, died in the Camp Hospital on ____________.
May I express my sincere sympathy on your bereavement. ____________ was admitted to the Hospital on ____________ with severe symptoms of exhaustion, complaining of difficulties in breathing and pains in the chest. Despite competent medication and devoted medical attention, it proved impossible, unfortunately, to keep the patient alive. The deceased voiced no final requests.

Camp Commandant, ____________

On 5th Street Bunko Certified Embalmer Catholic
Leans in his doorway drawing on a Natural Bloom Cigar.

He looks up the street. Even the Puerto Ricans are Jews
And the Chinese Laundry closes on Saturday.

– 12 –

Next door, outside the pink-fronted Bodega Hispano—

(A crying: you imagine
Some baby in its crib, wailing
As if it could foresee everything.
The crying subsides: you imagine
A mother or father clasping
The damned creature in their arms.
It breaks out again,
This time in a hair-raising shriek—ah,
The alleycat, in a pleasant guise,
In the darkness outside, in the alley,
Wauling, shrieking slowly in its blood.

Another, loftier shrieking
Drowns it out. It begins always
On the high note, over a clang of bells:
Hook & Ladder 11 with an explosion of mufflers
Crab-walking out of 5th Street,
Accelerating up the Avenue, siren
Sliding on the rounded distances
Returning fainter and fainter,
Like a bee looping away from where you lie in the grass.

The searchlights catch him at the topfloor window,
Trying to move, nailed in place by the shine.

The bells of Saint Brigid's
On Tompkins Square
Toll for someone who has died—
J'oïs la cloche de Serbonne,
Qui tousjours à neuf heures sonne
Le Salut que l'Ange prédit . . .

Expecting the visitation
You lie back on your bed,
The sounds outside

Must be outside. Here
Are only the dead spirituals
Turning back into prayers—
You rise on an elbow
To make sure they come from outside,
You hear nothing, you lay down
Your head on the pillow
Like a pick-up arm—
    swing low
            swing low
                    sweet
    lowsweet—)

—Carols of the Caribbean, plinkings of guitars.

- 13 -

The garbage disposal truck
Like a huge hunched animal
That sucks in garbage in the place
Where other animals evacuate it
Whines, as the cylinder in the rear
Threshes up the trash and garbage,
Where two men in rubber suits
(It must be raining outside)
Heap it in. The groaning motor
Rises in a whine as it grinds in
The garbage, and between-times
Groans. It whines and groans again.
All about it as it moves down
5th Street is the clatter of trashcans,
The crashes of them as the sanitary engineers
Bounce them on the sidewalk.

If it is raining outside
You can only tell by looking
In puddles, under the lifted streetlamps.

It would be the spring rain.

– 14 –

Behind the Power Station on 14th, the held breath
Of light, as God is a held breath, withheld,
Spreads the East River, into which fishes leak:
The brown sink or dissolve,
The white float out in shoals and armadas,
Even the gulls pass them up, pale
Bloated socks of riverwater and rotted seed,
That swirl on the tide, punched back
To the Hell Gate narrows, and on the ebb
Steam seaward, seeding the sea.

On the Avenue, through air tinted crimson
By neon over the bars, the rain is falling.
You stood once on Houston, among panhandlers and winos
Who weave the eastern ranges, learning to be free,
To not care, to be knocked flat and to get up clear-headed
Spitting the curses out. "Now be nice,"
The proprietor threatens; "Be nice," he cajoles.
"Fuck you," the bum shouts as he is hoisted again,
"God fuck your mother." (In the empty doorway,
Hunched on the empty crate, the crone gives no sign.)

That night a wildcat cab whined crosstown on 7th.
You knew even the traffic lights were made by God,
The red splashes growing dimmer the farther away
You looked, and away up at 14th, a few green stars;
And without sequence, and nearly all at once,
The red lights blinked into green,
And just before there was one complete Avenue of green,
The little green stars in the distance blinked.

It is night, and raining. You look down
Towards Houston in the rain, the living streets,
Where instants of transcendence
Drift in oceans of loathing and fear, like lanternfishes,
Or phosphorus flashings in the sea, or the feverish light
Skin is said to give off when the swimmer drowns at night.

From the blind gut Pitt to the East River of Fishes
The Avenue cobbles a swath through the discolored air,

A roadway of refuse from the teeming shores and ghettos
And the Caribbean Paradise, into the new ghetto and new paradise,
This God-forsaken Avenue bearing the initial of Christ
Through the haste and carelessness of the ages,
The sea standing in heaps, which keeps on collapsing,
Where the drowned suffer a C-change,
And remain the common poor.

Since Providence, for the realization of some unknown purpose, has seen fit to leave this dangerous people on the face of the earth, and did not destroy it . . .

Listen! The swish of the blood,
The sirens down the bloodpaths of the night,
Bone tapping on the bone, nerve-nets
Singing under the breath of sleep—

We scattered over the lonely seaways,
Over the lonely deserts did we run,
In dark lanes and alleys we did hide ourselves . . .

The heart beats without windows in its night,
The lungs put out the light of the world as they
Heave and collapse, the brain turns and rattles
In its own black axlegrease—

In the nighttime
Of the blood they are laughing and saying,
Our little lane, what a kingdom it was!

oi weih, oi weih

W. S. Merwin

« 1928 – »

WHITE GOAT, WHITE RAM

The gaiety of three winds is a game of green
Shining, of grey-and-gold play in the holly-bush
Among the rocks on the hill-side, and if ever
The earth was shaken, say a moment ago
Or whenever it came to be, only the leaves and the spread
Sea still betray it, trembling; and their tale betides
The faintest of small voices, almost still.
A road winds among the grey rocks, over the hill,
Arrives from out of sight, from nowhere we know,
Of an uncertain colour; and she stands at the side
Nearer the sea, not far from the brink, legs straddled wide
Over the swinging udder, her back and belly
Slung like a camp of hammocks, her head raised,
The narrow jaw grinding sideways, ears flapping sideways,
Eyes wide apart like the two moons of Mars
At their opposing. So broadly is she blind
Who has no names to see with: over her shoulder
She sees not summer, not the idea of summer,
But green meanings, shadows, the gold light of now, familiar,
The sense of long day-warmth, of sparse grass in the open
Game of the winds; an air that is plenitude,
Describing itself in no name; all known before,
Perceived many times before, yet not
Remembered, or at most felt as usual. Even the kids,
Grown now and gone, are forgotten,
As though by habit. And he on the other side
Of the road, hooves braced among spurge and asphodel,
Tears the grey grass at its roots, his massive horns
Tossing delicately, as by long habit, as by

Habit learned, or without other knowledge
And without question inherited, or found
As first he found the air, the first daylight, first milk at the tetter,
The paths, the pen, the seasons. They are white, these two,
As we should say those are white who remember nothing,
And we for our uses call that innocence,
So that our gracelessness may have the back of a goat
To ride away upon; so that when our supreme gesture
Of propitiation has obediently been raised
It may be the thicket-snared ram that dies instead of the son;
So even that we may frame the sense that is now
Into a starred figure of last things, of our own
End, and there by these beasts know ourselves
One from another: some to stay in the safety
Of the rock, but many on the other hand
To be dashed over the perilous brink. There is no need
Even that they should be gentle, for us to use them
To signify gentleness, for us to lift them as a sign
Invoking gentleness, conjuring by their shapes
The shape of our desire, which without them would remain
Without a form and nameless. For our uses
Also are a dumbness, a mystery,
Which like a habit stretches ahead of us
And was here before us; so, again, we use these
To designate what was before us, since we cannot
See it in itself, for who can recognize
And call by true names, familiarly, the place
Where before this he was, though for nine months
Or the world's full age he housed there? Yet it seems
That by such a road, arriving from out of sight,
From nowhere we know, we may have come, and these
Figure as shapes we may have been. Only, to them
The road is less than a road, though it divides them,
A bit of flat space merely, perhaps not even
A thing that leads elsewhere, except when they
Are driven along it, for direction is to them
The paths their own preference and kinds have made
And follow: routes through no convenience
And world of ours, but through their own sense
And mystery. Mark this; for though they assume
Now the awkward postures of illustrations

For all our parables, yet the mystery they stand in
Is still as far from what they signify
As from the mystery we stand in. It is the sign
We make of them, not they, that speaks from their dumbness
That our dumbness may speak. There in the thin grass
A few feet away they browse beyond words; for a mystery
Is that for which we have not yet received
Or made the name, the terms, that may enclose
And call it. And by virtue of such we stand beyond
Earthquake and wind and burning, and all the uncovenanted
Terror of becoming, and beyond the small voice; and on
Another hand, as it were a little above us
There are the angels. We are dumb before them, and move
In a different mystery; but may there be
Another road we do not see as a road: straight, narrow,
Or broad or the sector of a circle, or perhaps
All these, where without knowing it we stand
On one side or another? I have known such a way
But at moments only, and when it seemed I was driven
Along it, and along no other that my preference
Or kind had made. And of these others above us
We know only the whisper of an elusive sense,
Infrequent meanings and shadows, analogies
With light and the beating of wings. Yet now, perhaps only
A few feet away in the shaking leaves they wait
Beyond our words, beyond earthquake, whirlwind, fire,
And all the uncovenanted terror of becoming,
And beyond the small voice. Oh we cannot know and we are not
What we signify, but in what sign
May we be innocent, for out of our dumbness
We would speak for them, give speech to the mute tongues
Of angels. Listen: more than the sea's thunder
Foregathers in the grey cliffs; the roots of our hair
Stir like the leaves of the holly bush where now
Not games the wind ponders, but impatient
Glories, fire: and we go stricken suddenly
Humble, and the covering of our feet
Offends, for the ground where we find we stand is holy.

Part Four
GOD'S DEATH

Thomas Hardy

« 1840 – 1928 »

HAP

If but some vengeful god would call to me
From up the sky, and laugh: "Thou suffering thing,
Know that thy sorrow is my ecstasy,
That thy love's loss is my hate's profiting!"

Then would I bear it, clench myself, and die,
Steeled by the sense of ire unmerited;
Half-eased in that a Powerfuller than I
Had willed and meted me the tears I shed.

But not so. How arrives it joy lies slain,
And why unblooms the best hope ever sown?
—Crass Casualty obstructs the sun and rain,
And dicing Time for gladness casts a moan. . . .
These purblind Doomsters had as readily strown
Blisses about my pilgrimage as pain.

GOD'S FUNERAL

– I –

I saw a slowly-stepping train—
Lined on the brows, scoop-eyed and bent and hoar—
Following in files across a twilit plain
A strange and mystic form the foremost bore.

– II –

And by contagious throbs of thought
Or latent knowledge that within me lay
And had already stirred me, I was wrought
To consciousness of sorrow even as they.

– III –

The fore-borne shape, to my blurred eyes,
At first seemed man-like, and anon to change
To an amorphous cloud of marvelous size,
At times endowed with wings of glorious range.

– IV –

And this phantasmal variousness
Ever possessed it as they drew along:
Yet throughout all it symboled none the less
Potency vast and loving-kindness strong.

– V –

Almost before I knew I bent
Towards the moving columns without a word;
They, growing in bulk and numbers as they went,
Struck out sick thoughts that could be overheard:—

– VI –

"O man-projected Figure, of late
Imaged as we, thy knell who shall survive?
Whence came it we were tempted to create
One whom we can no longer keep alive?

– VII –

"Framing him jealous, fierce, at first,
We gave him justice as the ages rolled,
Will to bless those by circumstance accurst,
And long suffering, and mercies manifold.

– VIII –

"And, tricked by our own early dream
And need of solace, we grew self-deceived,

Our making soon our maker did we deem,
And what we had imagined we believed.

– IX –

"Till, in Time's stayless stealthy swing,
Uncompromising rude reality
Mangled the Monarch of our fashioning,
Who quavered, sank; and now has ceased to be.

– X –

"So, toward our myth's oblivion,
Darkling, and languid-lipped, we creep and grope
Sadlier than those who wept in Babylon,
Whose Zion was a still abiding hope.

– XI –

"How sweet it was in years far hied
To start the wheels of day with trustful prayer,
To lie down liegely at the eventide
And feel a blest assurance he was there!

– XII –

"And who or what shall fill his place?
Whither will wanderers turn distracted eyes
For some fixed star to stimulate their pace
Towards the goal of their enterprise?" . . .

– XIII –

Some in the background then I saw,
Sweet women, youths, men, all incredulous,
Who chimed: "This is a counterfeit of straw,
This requiem mockery! Still he lives to us!"

– XIV –

I could not buoy their faith: and yet
Many I had known: with all I sympathized;
And though struck speechless, I did not forget
That what was mourned for, I, too, long had prized.

– XV –

Still, how to bear such loss I deemed
The insistent question for each animate mind,
And gazing, to my growing sight there seemed
A pale yet positive gleam low down behind,

– XVI –

Whereof, to lift the general night,
A certain few who stood aloof had said,
"See you upon the horizon that small light—
Swelling somewhat?" Each mourner shook his head.

– XVII –

And they composed a crowd of whom
Some were right good, and many nigh the best. . . .
Thus dazed and puzzled 'twixt the gleam and gloom
Mechanically I followed with the rest.

NATURE'S QUESTIONING

When I look forth at dawning, pool,
Field, flock, and lonely tree,
All seem to gaze at me
Like chastened children sitting silent in a school;

Their faces dulled, constrained, and worn,
As though the master's ways
Through the long teaching days
Had cowed them till their early zest was overborne.

Upon them stirs in lippings mere
(As if once clear in call,
But now scarce breathed at all)—
"We wonder, ever wonder, why we find us here!

"Has some Vast Imbecility,
Mighty to build and blend,
But impotent to tend,
Framed us in jest, and left us now to hazardry?

"Or come we of an Automaton
Unconscious of our pains? . . .
Or are we live remains
Of Godhead dying downwards, brain and eye now gone?

"Or is it that some high Plan betides,
As yet not understood,
Of Evil stormed by Good,
We the Forlorn Hope over which Achievement strides?"

Thus things around. No answerer I . . .
Meanwhile the winds, and rains,
And Earth's old glooms and pains
Are still the same, and Life and Death are neighbours nigh.

IN CHURCH

"And now to God the Father," he ends,
And his voice thrills up to the topmost tiles:
Each listener chokes as he bows and bends,
And emotion pervades the crowded aisles.
Then the preacher glides to the vestry-door,
And shuts it, and thinks he is seen no more.

The door swings softly ajar meanwhile,
And a pupil of his in the Bible class,
Who adores him as one without gloss or guile,
Sees her idol stand with a satisfied smile
And re-enact at the vestry-glass
Each pulpit gesture in deft dumb-show
That had moved the congregation so.

IN TENEBRIS

– I –

Percussus sum sicut foenum,
et aruit cor meum.—PS. CI.

Wintertime nighs;
But my bereavement-pain
It cannot bring again:
Twice no one dies.

Flower-petals flee;
But, since it once hath been,
No more that severing scene
Can harrow me.

Birds faint in dread:
I shall not lose old strength
In the lone frost's black length:
Strength long since fled!

Leaves freeze to dun;
But friends can not turn cold
This season as of old
For him with none.

Tempests may scath;
But love can not make smart
Again this year his heart
Who no heart hath.

Black is night's cope;
But death will not appal
One who, past doubtings all,
Waits in unhope.

William Butler Yeats

« 1865 – 1939 »

A DIALOGUE OF SELF AND SOUL

– I –

MY SOUL. I summon to the winding ancient stair;
Set all your mind upon the steep ascent,
Upon the broken, crumbling battlement,
Upon the breathless starlit air,
Upon the star that marks the hidden pole;
Fix every wandering thought upon
That quarter where all thought is done:
Who can distinguish darkness from the soul?

MY SELF. The consecrated blade upon my knees
Is Sato's ancient blade, still as it was,
Still razor-keen, still like a looking-glass
Unspotted by the centuries;
That flowering, silken, old embroidery, torn
From some court-lady's dress and round
The wooden scabbard bound and wound,
Can, tattered, still protect, faded adorn.

MY SOUL. Why should the imagination of a man
Long past his prime remember things that are
Emblematical of love and war?
Think of ancestral night that can,
If but imagination scorn the earth
And intellect its wandering
To this and that and t' other thing,
Deliver from the crime of death and birth.

MY SELF. Montashigi, third of his family, fashioned it
Five hundred years ago, about it lie
Flowers from I know not what embroidery—
Heart's purple—and all these I set
For emblems of the day against the tower
Emblematical of the night,
And claim as by a soldier's right
A charter to commit the crime once more.

MY SOUL. Such fullness in that quarter overflows
And falls into the basin of the mind
That man is stricken deaf and dumb and blind,
For intellect no longer knows
Is from the *Ought*, or *Knower* from the *Known*—
That is to say, ascends to Heaven;
Only the dead can be forgiven;
But when I think of that my tongue's a stone.

– II –

MY SELF. A living man is blind and drinks his drop.
What matter if the ditches are impure?
What matter if I live it all once more?
Endure that toil of growing up;
The ignominy of boyhood; the distress
Of boyhood changing into man;
The unfinished man and his pain
Brought face to face with his own clumsiness;

The finished man among his enemies?—
How in the name of Heaven can he escape
That defiling and disfigured shape
The mirror of malicious eyes
Casts upon his eyes until at last
He thinks that shape must be his shape?
And what's the good of an escape
If honour find him in the wintry blast?

I am content to live it all again
And yet again, if it be life to pitch
Into the frog-spawn of a blind man's ditch,

A blind man battering blind men;
Or into that most fecund ditch of all,
The folly that man does
Or must suffer, if he woos
A proud woman not kindred of his soul.

I am content to follow to its source
Every event in action or in thought;
Measure the lot; forgive myself the lot!
When such as I cast out remorse
So great a sweetness flows into the breast
We must laugh and we must sing,
We are blest by everything,
Everything we look upon is blest.

THE SECOND COMING

Turning and turning in the widening gyre
The falcon cannot hear the falconer;
Things fall apart; the centre cannot hold;
Mere anarchy is loosed upon the world,
The blood-dimmed tide is loosed, and everywhere
The ceremony of innocence is drowned;
The best lack all conviction, while the worst
Are full of passionate intensity.

Surely some revelation is at hand;
Surely the Second Coming is at hand.
The Second Coming! Hardly are those words out
When a vast image out of *Spiritus Mundi*
Troubles my sight: somewhere in sands of the desert
A shape with lion body and the head of a man,
A gaze blank and pitiless as the sun,
Is moving its slow thighs, while all about it
Reel shadows of the indignant desert birds.
The darkness drops again; but now I know
That twenty centuries of stony sleep
Were vexed to nightmare by a rocking cradle,

And what rough beast, its hour come round at last,
Slouches towards Bethlehem to be born?

TWO SONGS FROM A PLAY

– I –

I SAW a staring virgin stand
Where holy Dionysus died,
And tear the heart out of his side,
And lay the heart upon her hand
And bear that beating heart away;
And then did all the Muses sing
Of Magnus Annus at the spring,
As though God's death were but a play.

Another Troy must rise and set,
Another lineage feed the crow,
Another Argo's painted prow
Drive to a flashier bauble yet.
The Roman Empire stood appalled:
It dropped the reigns of peace and war
When that fierce virgin and her Star
Out of the fabulous darkness called.

– II –

In pity for man's darkening thought
He walked that room and issued thence
In Galilean turbulence;
The Babylonian starlight brought
A fabulous, formless darkness in;
Odour of blood when Christ was slain
Made all Platonic tolerance vain
And vain all Doric discipline.

Everything that man esteems
Endures a moment or a day.
Love's pleasure drives his love away,

The painter's brush consumes his dreams;
The herald's cry, the soldier's tread
Exhaust his glory and his might:
Whatever flames upon the night
Man's own resinous heart has fed.

Wallace Stevens

« 1879 – 1955 »

SUNDAY MORNING

– I –

Complacencies of the peignoir, and late
Coffee and oranges in a sunny chair,
And the green freedom of a cockatoo
Upon a rug mingle to dissipate
The holy hush of ancient sacrifice.
She dreams a little, and she feels the dark
Encroachment of that old catastrophe,
As a calm darkens among water-lights.
The pungent oranges and bright, green wings
Seem things in some procession of the dead,
Winding across wide water, without sound.
The day is like wide water, without sound,
Stilled for the passing of her dreaming feet
Over the seas, to silent Palestine,
Dominion of the blood and sepulchre.

– II –

Why should she give her bounty to the dead?
What is divinity if it can come
Only in silent shadows and in dreams?
Shall she not find in comforts of the sun,
In pungent fruit and bright, green wings, or else
In any balm or beauty of the earth,
Things to be cherished like the thought of heaven?
Divinity must live within herself:
Passions of rain, or moods in falling snow;
Grievings in loneliness, or unsubdued

Elations when the forest blooms; gusty
Emotions on wet roads on autumn nights;
All pleasures and all pains, remembering
The bough of summer and the winter branch.
These are the measures destined for her soul.

– III –

Jove in the clouds had his inhuman birth.
No mother suckled him, no sweet land gave
Large-mannered motions to his mythy mind.
He moved among us, as a muttering king,
Magnificent, would move among his hinds,
Until our blood, commingling, virginal,
With heaven, brought such requital to desire
The very hinds discerned it, in a star.
Shall our blood fail? Or shall it come to be
The blood of paradise? And shall the earth
Seem all of paradise that we shall know?
The sky will be much friendlier then than now,
A part of labor and a part of pain,
And next in glory to enduring love,
Not this dividing and indifferent blue.

– IV –

She says, "I am content when wakened birds,
Before they fly, test the reality
Of misty fields, by their sweet questionings;
But when the birds are gone, and their warm fields
Return no more, where, then, is paradise?"
There is not any haunt of prophecy,
Nor any old chimera of the grave,
Neither the golden underground, nor isle
Melodious, where spirits gat them home,
Nor visionary south, nor cloudy palm
Remote on heaven's hill, that has endured
As April's green endures; or will endure
Like her remembrance of awakened birds,
Or her desire for June and evening, tipped
By the consummation of the swallow's wings.

– V –

She says, "But in contentment I still feel
The need of some imperishable bliss."
Death is the mother of beauty; hence from her,
Alone, shall come fulfillment to our dreams
And our desires. Although she strews the leaves
Of sure obliteration on our paths,
The path sick sorrow took, the many paths
Where triumph rang its brassy phrase, or love
Whispered a little out of tenderness,
She makes the willow shiver in the sun
For maidens who were wont to sit and gaze
Upon the grass, relinquished to their feet.
She causes boys to pile new plums and pears
On disregarded plate. The maidens taste
And stray impassioned in the littering leaves.

– VI –

Is there no change of death in paradise?
Does ripe fruit never fall? Or do the boughs
Hang always heavy in that perfect sky,
Unchanging, yet so like our perishing earth,
With rivers like our own that seek for seas
They never find, the same receding shores
That never touch with inarticulate pang?
Why set the pear upon those river-banks
Or spice the shores with odors of the plum?
Alas, that they should wear out colors there,
The silken weavings of our afternoons,
And pick the strings of our insipid lutes!
Death is the mother of beauty, mystical,
Within whose burning bosom we devise
Our earthly mothers waiting, sleeplessly.

– VII –

Supple and turbulent, a ring of men
Shall chant in orgy on a summer morn
Their boisterous devotion to the sun,
Not as a god, but as a god might be,

Naked among them, like a savage source.
Their chant shall be a chant of paradise,
Out of their blood, returning to the sky;
And in their chant shall enter, voice by voice,
The windy lake wherein their lord delights,
The trees, like serafin, and echoing hills,
That choir among themselves long afterward.
They shall know well the heavenly fellowship
Of men that perish and of summer morn.
And whence they came and whither they shall go
The dew upon their feet shall manifest.

– VIII –

She hears, upon that water without sound,
A voice that cries, "The tomb in Palestine
Is not the porch of spirits lingering.
It is the grave of Jesus, where he lay."
We live in an old chaos of the sun,
Or old dependency of day and night,
Or island solitude, unsponsored, free,
Of that wide water, inescapable.
Deer walk upon our mountains, and the quail
Whistle about us their spontaneous cries;
Sweet berries ripen in the wilderness;
And, in the isolation of the sky,
At evening, casual flocks of pigeons make
Ambiguous undulations as they sink,
Downward to darkness, on extended wings.

ESTHÉTIQUE DU MAL

– I –

He was at Naples writing letters home
And, between his letters, reading paragraphs
On the sublime. Vesuvius had groaned
For a month. It was pleasant to be sitting there,
While the sultriest fulgurations, flickering,

Cast corners in the glass. He could describe
The terror of the sound because the sound
Was ancient. He tried to remember the phrases: pain
Audible at noon, pain torturing itself,
Pain killing pain on the very point of pain.
The volcano trembled in another ether,
As the body trembles at the end of life.

It was almost time for lunch. Pain is human.
There were roses in the cool café. His book
Made sure of the most correct catastrophe.
Except for us, Vesuvius might consume
In solid fire the utmost earth and know
No pain (ignoring the cocks that crow us up
To die). This is a part of the sublime
From which we shrink. And yet, except for us,
The total past felt nothing when destroyed.

– II –

At a town in which acacias grew, he lay
On his balcony at night. Warblings became
Too dark, too far, too much the accents of
Afflicted sleep, too much the syllables
That would form themselves, in time, and communicate
The intelligence of his despair, express
What meditation never quite achieved.
The moon rose up as if it had escaped
His meditation. It evaded his mind.
It was part of a supremacy always
Above him. The moon was always free from him,
As night was free from him. The shadow touched
Or merely seemed to touch him as he spoke
A kind of elegy he found in space:

It is pain that is indifferent to the sky
In spite of the yellow of the acacias, the scent
Of them in the air still hanging heavily
In the hoary-hanging night. It does not regard
This freedom, this supremacy, and in
Its own hallucination never sees
How that which rejects it saves it in the end.

– III –

His firm stanzas hang like hives in hell
Or what hell was, since now both heaven and hell
Are one, and here, O terra infidel.

The fault lies with an over-human god,
Who by sympathy has made himself a man
And is not to be distinguished, when we cry

Because we suffer, our oldest parent, peer
Of the populace of the heart, the reddest lord,
Who has gone before us in experience.

If only he would not pity us so much,
Weaken our fate, relieve us of woe both great
And small, a constant fellow of destiny,

A too, too human god, self-pity's kin
And uncourageous genesis . . . It seems
As if the health of the world might be enough.

It seems as if the honey of common summer
Might be enough, as if the golden combs
Were part of a sustenance itself enough,

As if hell, so modified, had disappeared,
As if pain, no longer satanic mimicry,
Could be borne, as if we were sure to find our way.

– IV –

Livre de Toutes Sortes de Fleurs d'après Nature.
All sorts of flowers. That's the sentimentalist.
When B. sat down at the piano and made
A transparence in which we heard music, made music,
In which we heard transparent sounds, did he play
All sorts of notes? Or did he play only one
In an ecstasy of its associates,
Variations in the tones of a single sound,
The last, or sounds so single they seemed one?

And then that Spaniard of the rose, itself
Hot-hooded and dark-blooded, rescued the rose
From nature, each time he saw it, making it,
As he saw it, exist in his own especial eye.
Can we conceive of him as rescuing less,
As muffing the mistress for her several maids,
As foregoing the nakedest passion for barefoot
Philandering? . . . The genius of misfortune
Is not a sentimentalist. He is
That evil, that evil in the self, from which
In desperate hallow, rugged gesture, fault
Falls out on everything: the genius of
The mind, which is our being, wrong and wrong,
The genius of the body, which is our world,
Spent in the false engagements of the mind.

– v –

Softly let all true sympathizers come,
Without the inventions of sorrow or the sob
Beyond invention. Within what we permit,
Within the actual, the warm, the near,
So great a unity, that it is bliss,
Ties us to those we love. For this familiar,
This brother even in the father's eye,
This brother half-spoken in the mother's throat
And these regalia, these things disclosed,
These nebulous brilliancies in the smallest look
Of the being's deepest darling, we forego
Lament, willingly forfeit the ai-ai
Of parades in the obscurer selvages.

Be near me, come closer, touch my hand, phrases
Compounded of dear relation, spoken twice,
Once by the lips, once by the services
Of central sense, these minutiae mean more
Than clouds, benevolences, distant heads.
These are within what we permit, in-bar
Exquisite in poverty against the suns
Of ex-bar, in-bar retaining attributes
With which we vested, once, the golden forms
And the damasked memory of the golden forms

And ex-bar's flowers and fire of the festivals
Of the damasked memory of the golden forms,
Before we were wholly human and knew ourselves.

– VI –

The sun, in clownish yellow, but not a clown,
Brings the day to perfection and then fails. He dwells
In a consummate prime, yet still desires
A further consummation. For the lunar month
He makes the tenderest research, intent
On a transmutation which, when seen, appears
To be askew. And space is filled with his
Rejected years. A big bird pecks at him
For food. The big bird's bony appetite
Is as insatiable as the sun's. The bird
Rose from an imperfection of its own
To feed on the yellow bloom of the yellow fruit
Dropped down from turquoise leaves. In the landscape of
The sun, its grossest appetite becomes less gross,
Yet, when corrected, has its curious lapses,
Its glitters, its divinations of serene
Indulgence out of all celestial sight.

The sun is the country wherever he is. The bird
In the brightest landscape downwardly revolves
Disdaining each astringent ripening,
Evading the point of redness, not content
To repose in an hour or season or long era
Of the country colors crowding against it, since
The yellow grassman's mind is still immense,
Still promises perfections cast away.

– VII –

How red the rose that is the soldier's wound,
The wounds of many soldiers, the wounds of all
The soldiers that have fallen, red in blood,
The soldier of time grown deathless in great size.

A mountain in which no ease is ever found,
Unless indifference to deeper death

Is ease, stands in the dark, a shadows' hill,
And there the soldier of time has deathless rest.

Concentric circles of shadows, motionless
Of their own part, yet moving on the wind,
Form mystical convolutions in the sleep
Of time's red soldier deathless on his bed.

The shadows of his fellows ring him round
In the high night, the summer breathes for them
Its fragrance, a heavy somnolence, and for him,
For the soldier of time, it breathes a summer sleep,

In which his wound is good because life was.
No part of him was ever part of death.
A woman smoothes her forehead with her hand
And the soldier of time lies calm beneath that stroke.

– VIII –

The death of Satan was a tragedy
For the imagination. A capital
Negation destroyed him in his tenement
And, with him, many blue phenomena.
It was not the end he had foreseen. He knew
That his revenge created filial
Revenges. And negation was eccentric.
It had nothing of the Julian thunder-cloud:
The assassin flash and rumble . . . He was denied.
Phantoms, what have you left? What underground?
What place in which to be is not enough
To be? You go, poor phantoms, without place
Like silver in the sheathing of the sight,
As the eye closes . . . How cold the vacancy
When the phantoms are gone and the shaken realist
First sees reality. The mortal no
Has its emptiness and tragic expirations.
The tragedy, however, may have begun,
Again, in the imagination's new beginning,
In the yes of the realist spoken because he must
Say yes, spoken because under every no
Lay a passion for yes that had never been broken.

– IX –

Panic in the face of the moon—round effendi
Or the phosphored sleep in which he walks abroad
Or the majolica dish heaped up with phosphored fruit
That he sends ahead, out of the goodness of his heart,
To anyone that comes—panic, because
The moon is no longer these nor anything
And nothing is left but comic ugliness
Or a lustred nothingness. Effendi, he
That has lost the folly of the moon becomes
The prince of the proverbs of pure poverty.
To lose sensibility, to see what one sees,
As if sight had not its own miraculous thrift,
To hear only what one hears, one meaning alone,
As if the paradise of meaning ceased
To be paradise, it is this to be destitute.
This is the sky divested of its fountains.
Here in the west indifferent crickets chant
Through our indifferent crises. Yet we require
Another chant, an incantation, as in
Another and later genesis, music
That buffets the shapes of its possible halcyon
Against the haggardie . . . A loud, large water
Bubbles up in the night and drowns the crickets' sound.
It is a declaration, a primitive ecstasy,
Truth's favors sonorously exhibited.

– X –

He had studied the nostalgias. In these
He sought the most grossly maternal, the creature
Who most fecundly assuaged him, the softest
Woman with a vague moustache and not the mauve
Maman. His anima liked its animal
And liked it unsubjugated, so that home
Was a return to birth, a being born
Again in the savagest severity,
Desiring fiercely, the child of a mother fierce
In his body, fiercer in his mind, merciless
To accomplish the truth in his intelligence.
It is true there were other mothers, singular

In form, lovers of heaven and earth, she-wolves
And forest tigresses and women mixed
With the sea. These were fantastic. There were homes
Like things submerged with their englutted sounds,
That were never wholly still. The softest woman,
Because she is as she was, reality,
The gross, the fecund, proved him against the touch
Of impersonal pain. Reality explained.
It was the last nostalgia: that he
Should understand. That he might suffer or that
He might die was the innocence of living, if life
Itself was innocent. To say that it was
Disentangled him from sleek ensolacings.

– XI –

Life is a bitter aspic. We are not
At the centre of a diamond. At dawn,
The paratroopers fall and as they fall
They mow the lawn. A vessel sinks in waves
Of people, as big bell-billows from its bell
Bell-bellow in the village steeple. Violets,
Great tufts, spring up from buried houses
Of poor, dishonest people, for whom the steeple,
Long since, rang out farewell, farewell, farewell.

Natives of poverty, children of malheur,
The gaiety of language is our seigneur.

A man of bitter appetite despises
A well-made scene in which paratroopers
Select adieux; and he despises this:
A ship that rolls on a confected ocean,
The weather pink, the wind in motion; and this:
A steeple that tip-tops the classic sun's
Arrangements; and the violets' exhumo.
The tongue caresses these exacerbations.
They press it as epicure, distinguishing
Themselves from its essential savor,
Like hunger that feeds on its own hungriness.

– XII –

He disposes the world in categories, thus:
The peopled and the unpeopled. In both, he is
Alone. But in the peopled world, there is,
Besides the people, his knowledge of them. In
The unpeopled, there is his knowledge of himself.
Which is more desperate in the moments when
The will demands that what he thinks be true?

Is it himself in them that he knows or they
In him? If it is himself in them, they have
No secret from him. If it is they in him,
He has no secret from them. This knowledge
Of them and of himself destroys both worlds,
Except when he escapes from it. To be
Alone is not to know them or himself.

This creates a third world without knowledge,
In which no one peers, in which the will makes no
Demands. It accepts whatever is as true,
Including pain, which, otherwise, is false.
In the third world, then, there is no pain. Yes, but
What lover has one in such rocks, what woman,
However known, at the centre of the heart?

– XIII –

It may be that one life is a punishment
For another, as the son's life for the father's.
But that concerns the secondary characters.
It is a fragmentary tragedy
Within the universal whole. The son
And the father alike and equally are spent,
Each one, by the necessity of being
Himself, the unalterable necessity
Of being this unalterable animal.
This force of nature in action is the major
Tragedy. This is destiny unperplexed,
The happiest enemy. And it may be
That in his Mediterranean cloister a man,
Reclining, eased of desire, establishes

The visible, a zone of blue and orange
Versicolorings, establishes a time
To watch the fire-feinting sea and calls it good,
The ultimate good, sure of a reality
Of the longest meditation, the maximum,
The assassin's scene. Evil in evil is
Comparative. The assassin discloses himself,
The force that destroys us is disclosed, within
This maximum, an adventure to be endured
With the politest helplessness. Ay-mi!
One feels its action moving in the blood.

– XIV –

Victor Serge said, "I followed his argument
With the blank uneasiness which one might feel
In the presence of a logical lunatic."
He said it of Konstantinov. Revolution
Is the affair of logical lunatics.
The politics of emotion must appear
To be an intellectual structure. The cause
Creates a logic not to be distinguished
From lunacy . . . One wants to be able to walk
By the lake at Geneva and consider logic:
To think of the logicians in their graves
And of the worlds of logic in their great tombs.
Lakes are more reasonable than oceans. Hence,
A promenade amid the grandeurs of the mind,
By a lake, with clouds like lights among great tombs,
Gives one a blank uneasiness, as if
One might meet Konstantinov, who would interrupt
With his lunacy. He would not be aware of the lake.
He would be the lunatic of one idea
In a world of ideas, who would have all the people
Live, work, suffer and die in that idea
In a world of ideas. He would not be aware of the clouds,
Lighting the martyrs of logic with white fire.
His extreme of logic would be illogical.

– XV –

The greatest poverty is not to live
In a physical world, to feel that one's desire
Is too difficult to tell from despair. Perhaps,
After death, the non-physical people, in paradise,
Itself non-physical, may, by chance, observe
The green corn gleaming and experience
The minor of what we feel. The adventurer
In humanity has not conceived of a race
Completely physical in a physical world.
The green corn gleams and the metaphysicals
Lie sprawling in majors of the August heat,
The rotund emotions, paradise unknown.
This is the thesis scrivened in delight,
The reverberating psalm, the right chorale.

One might have thought of sight, but who could think
Of what it sees, for all the ill it sees?
Speech found the ear, for all the evil sound,
But the dark italics it could not propound.
And out of what one sees and hears and out
Of what one feels, who could have thought to make
So many selves, so many sensuous worlds,
As if the air, the mid-day air, was swarming
With the metaphysical changes that occur,
Merely in living as and where we live.

Theodore Roethke

« 1908 – 1963 »

MEDITATIONS OF AN OLD WOMAN

First Meditation

– 1 –

On love's worst ugly day,
The weeds hiss at the edge of the field,
The small winds make their chilly indictments.
Elsewhere, in houses, even pails can be sad;
While stones loosen on the obscure hillside,
And a tree tilts from its roots,
Toppling down an embankment.

The spirit moves, but not always upward,
While animals eat to the north,
And the shale slides an inch in the talus,
The bleak wind eats at the weak plateau,
And the sun brings joy to some.
But the rind, often, hates the life within.

How can I rest in the days of my slowness?
I've become a strange piece of flesh,
Nervous and cold, bird-furtive, whiskery,
With a cheek soft as a hound's ear.
What's left is light as a seed;
I need an old crone's knowing.

– 2 –

Often I think of myself as riding—
Alone, on a bus through western country.
I sit above the back wheels, where the jolts are hardest,
And we bounce and sway along toward the midnight,
The lights tilting up, skyward, as we come over a little rise,

Then down, as we roll like a boat from a wave-crest.
All journeys, I think, are the same:
The movement is forward, after a few wavers,
And for a while we are all alone,
Busy, obvious with ourselves,
The drunken soldier, the old lady with her peppermints;
And we ride, we ride, taking the curves
Somewhat closer, the trucks coming
Down from behind the last ranges,
Their black shapes breaking past;
And the air claps between us,
Blasting the frosted windows,
And I seem to go backward,
Backward in time:

Two song sparrows, one within a greenhouse,
Shuttling its throat while perched on a wind-vent,
And another, outside, in the bright day,
With a wind from the west and the trees all in motion.
One sang, then the other,
The songs tumbling over and under the glass,
And the men beneath them wheeling in dirt to the cement benches,
The laden wheelbarrows creaking and swaying,
And the up-spring of the plank when a foot left the runway.

Journey within a journey:
The ticket mislaid or lost, the gate
Inaccessible, the boat always pulling out
From the rickety wooden dock,
The children waving;
Or two horses plunging in snow, their lines tangled,
A great wooden sleigh careening behind them,
Swerving up a steep embankment.
For a moment they stand above me,
Their black skins shuddering:
Then they lurch forward,
Lunging down a hillside.

– 3 –

As when silt drifts and sifts down through muddy pond-water,
Settling in small beads around weeds and sunken branches,

And one crab, tentative, hunches himself before moving along the bottom,
Grotesque, awkward, his extended eyes looking at nothing in particular,
Only a few bubbles loosening from the ill-matched tentacles,
The tail and smaller legs slipping and sliding slowly backward—
So the spirit tries for another life,
Another way and place in which to continue;
Or a salmon, tired, moving up a shallow stream,
Nudges into a back-eddy, a sandy inlet,
Bumping against sticks and bottom-stones, then swinging
Around, back into the tiny maincurrent, the rush of brownish-white water,
Still swimming forward—
So, I suppose, the spirit journeys.

– 4 –

I have gone into the waste lonely places
Behind the eye; the lost acres at the edge of smoky cities.
What's beyond never crumbles like an embankment,
Explodes like a rose, or thrusts wings over the Caribbean.
There are no pursuing forms, faces on walls:
Only the motes of dust in the immaculate hallways,
The darkness of falling hair, the warnings from lint and spiders,
The vines graying to a fine powder.
There is no riven tree, or lamb dropped by an eagle.
There are still times, morning and evening:
The cerulean, high in the elm,
Thin and insistent as a cicada,
And the far phoebe, singing,
The long plaintive notes floating down,
Drifting through leaves, oak and maple,
Or the whippoorwill, along the smoky ridges,
A single bird calling and calling;
A fume reminds me, drifting across wet gravel;
A cold wind comes over stones;
A flame, intense, visible,
Plays over the dry pods,
Runs fitfully along the stubble,
Moves over the field,
Without burning.
    In such times, lacking a god,
    I am still happy.

John Ciardi

« 1916 – »

IN THE STONEWORKS

In the stoneworks under God, the broken statuary
formed ranks like an army in storage. Spiders wove
halos for the headless. Detailed worms
lay rusted shut in the ringbolts, link by link.

Upstairs, in the tree-light, shapes blurred. Briar
had taken the stone stumps, grass the floor plan.
Threee first trunks still shored a pediment,
and there Gods, weathered featureless, enacted

half-gestures over the gravels of themselves.
But swallows had fouled the inscriptions,
and out of hanging muds the fledglings flamed,
ravenous and shrill. The air creaked with their hunger.

In the sky, an ice-age coiled, and let fall light.
What could be light. What was light-as-it-is,
passing the time it takes till even the stoneworks
under the stoneworks stand bare to the unmade day.

Philip Larkin

« 1922 – »

CHURCH GOING

Once I am sure there's nothing going on
I step inside, letting the door thud shut.
Another church: matting, seats, and stone,
And little books; sprawlings of flowers, cut
For Sunday, brownish now; some brass and stuff
Up at the holy end; the small neat organ;
And a tense, musty, unignorable silence,
Brewed God knows how long. Hatless, I take off
My cycle-clips in awkward reverence,

Move forward, run my hand around the font.
From where I stand, the roof looks almost new—
Cleaned, or restored? Someone would know: I don't.
Mounting the lectern, I peruse a few
Hectoring large-scale verses, and pronounce
'Here endeth' much more loudly than I'd meant.
The echoes snigger briefly. Back at the door
I sign the book, donate an Irish sixpence,
Reflect the place was not worth stopping for.

Yet stop I did: in fact I often do,
And always end much at a loss like this,
Wondering what to look for; wondering, too,
When churches fall completely out of use
What we shall turn them into, if we shall keep
A few cathedrals chronically on show,
Their parchment, plate and pyx in locked cases,
And let the rest rent-free to rain and sheep.
Shall we avoid them as unlucky places?

Or, after dark, will dubious women come
To make their children touch a particular stone;
Pick simples for a cancer; or in some
Advised night see walking a dead one?
Power of some sort or other will go on
In games, in riddles, seemingly at random;
But superstition, like belief, must die,
And what remains when disbelief has gone?
Grass, weedy pavement, brambles, buttress, sky,

A shape less recognisable each week,
A purpose more obscure. I wonder who
Will be the last, the very last, to seek
This place for what it was; one of the crew
That tap and jot and know what rood-lofts were?
Some ruin-bibber, randy for antique,
Or Christmas-addict, counting on a whiff
Of gown-and-bands and organ-pipes and myrrh?
Or will he be my representative,

Bored, uninformed, knowing the ghostly silt
Dispersed, yet tending to this cross of ground
Through suburb scrub because it held unspilt
So long and equably what since is found
Only in separation—marriage, and birth,
And deaths, and thoughts of these—for whom was built
This special shell? For, though I've no idea
What this accoutred frowsty barn is worth,
It pleases me to stand in silence here;

A serious house on serious earth it is,
In whose blent air all our compulsions meet,
Are recognised, and robed as destinies.
And that much never can be obsolete,
Since someone will forever be surprising
A hunger in himself to be more serious,
And gravitating with it to this ground,
Which, he once heard, was proper to grow wise in,
If only that so many dead lie round.

Robert Pack

« 1929 – »

MY HOUSE

Still poised, as if in prayer,
The bleached hermit-crab,
Crusted in geologic quiet,
Has stopped going backwards. Sunlight
Falls, purified
Of memory. And you, the god
Who never was, still listen.
At odd hours, from under stones,
You called me back where slow moss
Mouthed, "rest here, rest here,"
From lace, grandmother's veil,
Or, when the starred snow wheeled,
From filaments, from window-sills.

Envy of those with a cause to die for,
Those who count their enemies,
Free to murder, free to dream
Of better things to come;
Envy of the mole, peeping
Through the snow for seeds,
Who liked not seeing what he could not see;
Of birds stuffed bright to death
With three young years sung in their throats;
Of grass, growing from skulls
Like mock hair, drying the slime of eyes,
Sealing wax chambers of turned-in ears;
Envy of monumental stone,
Secure and peaceful—envy
Because, needing something beyond

To live for, in your good name, god,
Something in me wished
To murder and to die.

It was you turned me against my father
When his tricked heart sucked like a fish
At the bland air; you cheated
My grief as the blue veins rose
On the backs of my mother's hands;
It was you when webbing wind
Gobbled at dust, spinning
In unfed corners of their house.

Now, on my boulder-strewn, green hill,
Happy in my nourished house,
A wife, two dogs, children to come,
Hating what twenty Christian
Centuries have willed,
My last cramped thoughts, sifting seaward,
Lock in my guarded hours:
Shoulders hunch to a shell;
My elbows bend to tentacles.
And there I am, dead
A silent million years, all salted clean,
With you still listening.

ADAM ON HIS WAY HOME

For Daniel and Janet Newman

By the wayside, three crows sat on a cross.
It was a long journey back, the rank road
Passable only on foot, and his memories
Were little consolation. What good was past

Happiness or, for that matter, past
Suffering? Dignity, in these limp days,
Was poor payment for leaky eyes. There was nothing
To set against thin death as in the old times.

The buzzard sun flapped in his face, rattling
The stones in his wrists, his elbows, his ribs, with a tide
Of pebbles mumbling in his humbled ears,
"Nothing, nothing." Between his toes lizards

Ran where nails cracked and peeled. And this
Was not the mud of penitence, but decay.
This was the limp time, with cramped air clotted
In his nose, his tasteless tongue shrivelled dry as rope.

And then, although he was not superstitious,
It happened, as he always knew it would.
Beneath the first fruit tree, a draped figure,
Featureless, shaped as if by wind on water,

Drew him down gently, whispering, "Come to me,
I am the one!" His forked breath parted the wind,
Like clothes fallen away, and there she lay
Smiling with his eyes, his lips, and his fierce tongue,

All grown young: his forked breath breathed apart
Her foaming water-thighs, with the dark clutched between,
His own, his calling dark, smelling of home,
Where he leapt in the final spasm of first love.

Ted Hughes

« 1930 – »

PIBROCH

The sea cries with its meaningless voice,
Treating alike its dead and its living,
Probably bored with the appearance of heaven
After so many millions of nights without sleep,
Without purpose, without self-deception.

Stone likewise. A pebble is imprisoned
Like nothing in the Universe.
Created for black sleep. Or growing
Conscious of the sun's red spot occasionally,
Then dreaming it is the foetus of God.

Over the stone rushes the wind,
Able to mingle with nothing,
Like the hearing of the blind stone itself.
Or turns, as if the stone's mind came feeling
A fantasy of directions.

Drinking the sea and eating the rock
A tree struggles to make leaves—
An old woman fallen from space
Unprepared for these conditions.
She hangs on, because her mind's gone completely.

Minute after minute, aeon after aeon,
Nothing lets up or develops.
And this is neither a bad variant nor a tryout.
This is where the staring angels go through.
This is where all the stars bow down.

Jon Silkin

« 1930 – »

FURNISHED LIVES

I have been walking to-day
Where the sour children of London's poor sleep
Pressed close to the unfrosted glare,
Torment lying closed in tenement,
Of the clay fire; I
Have watched their whispering souls fly straight to God:

'O Lord, please give to us
A dinner-service, austere, yet gay: like snow
When swans are on it; Bird,
Unfold your wings until like a white smile
You fill this mid-white room.
I have balanced myself on the needle of the Strand where

Each man and maiden turn,
On the deliberate hour of the cock
As if two new risen souls,
Through the cragged landscape in each other's eyes.
But where lover upon lover
Should meet,—where sheet, and pillow, and eiderdown

Should frolic and breathe
As dolphins on the stylized crown of the sea
Their pale cerements lie.
They tread with chocolate souls and paper hands,
They walk into that room
Your gay and daffodil smile has never seen:

Not to love's pleasant feast
They go, in the mutations of the night,

But to their humiliations
Paled as a swan's dead feather scorched in the sun.
I have been walking to-day
Among the newly paper-crowned, among these

Whose casual, paper body
Is crushed between fate's fingers and the platter;
But Sir, their perpetual fire
Was not stubbed out, folded on brass or stone
Extinguished in the dark,
But burns with the drear dampness of cut flowers.

I cannot hear their piped
Cry. These souls have no players. They have resigned
The vivid performance of their world.
And your world, Lord,
Has now become
Like a dumb winter show, held in one room,

Which must now reek of age
Before you have retouched its lips with such straight fire
As through your stony earth
Burns with ferocious tears in the world's eyes;
Church-stone, door-knocker and polished railway lines
Move in their separate dumb way
So why not these lives:
I ask you often, but you never say?

George Starbuck

« 1931 – »

POEMS FROM A FIRST YEAR IN BOSTON

To Jonathan Edwards, d. 1758

– IV. AUTUMN: PROGRESS REPORT –

Becalmed in old Back Bay's dead water sulk
the square four-storey barges, hulk to hulk.
These increments, so brusquely set aside
by the busy longshore muscle of the tide,
nurse the cut glint of chandelier and cup
like geodes: here Cathay lies silted up,
where tides of trade once moved: old weather eyes
look from the mansard portholes sans surmise.
Sans tooth, sans claw, late blood-competitors
hold in the faces of inheritors
a tight precarious old man's embrace.

Whaddaya do for action in this place?
Taxicabs scuttle by on the wet streets.
I weave with two sweet ladies out of the Ritz,
stare at the Garden pond.
                                        Old pioneer,
Jonathan Edwards, did you stop off here
where marsh birds skittered, and a longboat put
its weed-grown bones to pasture at the foot
of Beacon, close on Charles Street? And see then,
already sick with glut, this hill of men?
And even there, see God? And in this marsh,
and in the wood beyond, grace of a harsh
God? And in these crabbed streets, unto the mid-
mire of them, God? Old Soul, you said you did.

It's still the same congested spit of land—
Dry Heaven's devil's-island, where the banned
gods of the blood's regime still play at court
in the stripped palatial prisons of the heart.
Poor pagan spooks, so gently spoken of
in Boston—brainwashed beggar-ghosts of love
so painsfully, as if we knew such gods,
trying our neoclassical facades—

Prayer without praise. Glut in the atrium.
Jonathan, praise *is* said where the heart's drum
carries from camp to camp through jungles of
the entwined dark flesh, and the beat of love,
forcing that forest, overflows the sky.

Vegetal flesh, huge-bosomed, fills the eye
on Washington Street. Portly drummers fall,
their clotted hearts into their hands, on Wall,
unsounded and unsung. You had your grand
God at your heart; you trembled in his hand;
you magnified his universe, his voice

cupped in your ear by farthest space: "Rejoice
that you know not!" And knew, curled like God's spit
in dust, his meanest Incarnation: it
can be State Street and Monday Noon: it may
be a shape to damn: passersby might say
Satan the Tempter put that quaking on
to bend your hand toward his halt heart, alone
of all those godly—
                                        God what else but flout
a Kingdom we can never know, cast out
with all our flesh and blood before our birth?
What else but turn to this hard island, earth,
and dig for its downed gods? God I could laugh,
so many pray; and yet—
                                              I have seen half
the sculpted heads of Boston make the face
of one caged lion of a man their place
of weary battle: every day again
he must survive them all—the lettered men,

the men of means, the men of parts and shares—
and if he seeks God's peace instead of theirs,
God rest him for it: though I no more can
stomach your God than you my faith in man,
I too must worship blindly, Jonathan.

Indexes

Index of Poets

Index of Titles

Index of First Lines